"Don't Be Sad
When I'm Gone"

"Don't Be Sad When I'm Gone"

A Memoir of Loss and Healing in Buenos Aires

BEATRIZ DUJOVNE

Foreword by NEIL J. SKOLNICK, PH.D.

Toplight

Jefferson, North Carolina

ISBN (print) 978-1-4766-8428-4 ∞
ISBN (ebook) 978-1-4766-4185-0

LIBRARY OF CONGRESS AND BRITISH LIBRARY
CATALOGUING DATA ARE AVAILABLE

Front cover image © 2020 Photographee.eu/Shutterstock

Printed in the United States of America

Toplight is an imprint of McFarland & Company, Inc., Publishers

*Box 611, Jefferson, North Carolina 28640
www.toplightbooks.com*

To Carlos

Acknowledgments

Neither this book nor the healing process it portrays would have been possible without my therapeutic sessions with Dr. Enrique Novelli. I wish to thank him for his impeccable technique and his personal warmth in helping me walk the road of grief as I needed to do it, and for his consent to publish excerpts and representations of our sessions.

I am honored and delighted to thank professor and practicing psychoanalyst Neil J. Skolnick, Ph.D., who was receptive to reviewing this book and agreed to supply the Foreword. I also wish to thank Megan Devine, M.A., grief specialist, for reviewing my manuscript while it was in the final production phase before publication. To Natalie Foreman, my editor at McFarland, I wish to express my thanks for seeing this project through its final stages to publication.

Finally, my heartfelt gratitude goes to my editor Jake Spatz for his flawless job helping me throughout the making of this book, and for going above and beyond his duties in offering sensitive companionship and support during some hard writing moments.

Table of Contents

Foreword
by Neil J. Skolnick, Ph.D.

Beatriz Dujovne begins with "This book is about a woman in grief," which, to be sure, it is. And yet it is about so very much more. The "more" is what I will attempt to illuminate in this Foreword. Indeed, she asks her readers to accompany her through the torturous, poignant and intimate account of her recovery from the death of her beloved husband Carlos. A death that others who have already endured the shattering demise of a loved one will recognize as having abruptly deposited them on an altered planet, one that appears vaguely familiar but where nothing is the same. Everything, her relationships, her work, the landscape, is now cast in new light, new shadings demanding to be comprehended but which appear hopelessly confusing, frightening, alien and stretching endlessly into a future lacking clear guidelines, if not meaning. She states at the outset:

> My hope is that the narrative in this book can offer empathic resonance and new insights, and can open new paths to individuals grieving or facing the oncoming death of loved ones. At one point, I thought I wasn't suffering enough—a thought which deserves to cross no person's mind. *There is no script for everyone.*

There is no script for everyone. This idea serves as one of the defining themes running throughout the book. In stark contrast to the now somewhat formulaic and widely accepted lock-step process of grieving, as laid out by Kübler-Ross (1969), Beatriz repeatedly stresses that one size does not fit all. Each person's grieving process is unique, shaped by the unique circumstances of each person's narrative, external and internal. Researchers and statisticians typically strive to eliminate error variance (in essence, individual differences) in their quest to define the categorical. Beatriz makes a clarion call for research efforts exploring grief to highlight and explore the roots of error variance as a road to understanding each griever's unique experiential plight. I've no doubt that envisioning grieving as a process unique to each griever must come as a great relief to those who have lost a loved one and are not responding in prescribed, lock-step, or societally-sanctioned ways. Her experience should also serve as a relief to those clinicians who work with grief in a therapeutic capacity. Of great importance, she wisely claims:

> Inside you there is your own road map which you may not be able to read on your own. Therapy can give you that other set of eyes, that other set of ears, that other human contact—the most natural way to find ourselves and our sense of wholeness.

As a psychologist herself, Beatriz specifically refers to a psychoanalytically informed therapy. She opted for this form of psychotherapy because, again, in her own words:

> Why did I choose psychoanalysis? I am a psychologist trained in both countries [the United States and Argentina—her country of origin]. Among all the methods of therapy, I prefer the psychoanalytic one that brings unconscious emotions and conflicts into present awareness, as opposed to the cognitive or behavioral methods that navigate consciousness, which are used by most therapists in the States. Self-help books that offer advice to the grieving person do not resonate with me very much. Both of those tools scratch the surface—they don't reach down to the level of raw emotion. Sure, many people in the United States think they should be grieving by themselves. Chances are they could do it faster and better with the assistance of psychotherapy.

She invites us into the private, intimate psychoanalytically oriented psychotherapy sessions she underwent in Buenos Aires to help with her grief. She sought therapy with a humane and talented psychoanalyst. These sessions have been reconstructed to present the reader with a more linear account than the often circular, loop-de-loop actual process of psychotherapy. They provide the backbone of her narrative and pull the reader through her process of recovery. I stated at the outset that this book is about much more than a woman in grief. The reader will discover it is also an homage to the efficacy of psychoanalysis in addressing a more comprehensive understanding of the human condition. Much maligned by

Foreword by Neil J. Skolnick, Ph.D.

American psychotherapists working from American sensibilities of pragmatism, cost cutting and a reliance on "show me" empiricism, psychoanalysis has been embraced by Argentinians as the treatment of choice for manifold problems in living. Argentina is known to have a higher *per capita* number of psychoanalysts than any other country in the world (2020, *New York Times*).[1] A psychoanalyst myself, I presumptuously take on the mantle of an honorary Argentinian and wish more Americans would recognize, as do the Argentinians, its power to heal. I am not against other forms of psychological treatment and indeed psychoanalysis has its own limitations with certain disorders. However, when working with such a complicated, all encompassing, at times mysterious process like grieving, a psychoanalytic approach is what I too find most efficacious in helping a grieving person regain ballast and meaning in their lives as they return to a now permanently altered world.

Included in no small measure in the "much more" that I claim this book offers is that it transcends death and grief and turns out to be equally about life. And ground zero for Beatriz's life force is where it was originally given birth and form, her native home of Buenos Aires. We follow her to Buenos Aires from her present home in Portland, Oregon, where she journeys to rekindle her life. Sprinkled between her therapy sessions, she proudly shows us the Buenos Aires that long ago took up permanent residence in her blood. She takes us to her favorite eateries, through the dappled light of her favorite gardens with their resplendent bursts of colorful flowers, to the cacophony of architecture, grand and not so grand, boulevards, backstreets and stores that populate her hometown. We witness those special spots where her love affair with Carlos bloomed and took hold. But it is not just these iconic images of her physical landscape, it is equally the connections to the people she meets up with in these nostalgically saturated places, from the waiters, store owners, old friends and family members (hers and Carlos') that also play a significant role in the

---

1. The number of practicing psychologists in Argentina has been surging, to 196 per 100,000 people last year, according to a study by Modesto Alonso, a psychologist and researcher, from 145 per 100,000 people in 2008. That compares with about 27 psychologists per 100,000 people in the United States, according to the American Psychological Association.

resolution of her grief. The verdant flora and human fauna provide a swirl of colorful smoke and fragrant odors and delicious food that weave organically throughout, like the vapors that congealed to form primitive life forms on our planet. They all conspire to give her life renewed substance and value. In the love she cherishes for Buenos Aires and its *Portenos*[2] she garners the strength to relinquish her anguish and charge intrepidly into a new life. And by the by, being seduced into falling in love with the magical charms of Buenos Aires is a special treat for the reader as well.

Portenos are passionate about their tribal dance, the tango. It would be difficult to underestimate the role that the tango figures in Beatriz's recovery. In addition to being a psychologist, she is a dancer and has written extensively about the tango,[3] Argentina's immeasurable cultural contribution to the world. In my opinion the tango is to dance what psychoanalysis is to psychology. It is particularly suited to express the depths and nuances of the human experience. Tango *gypsies* cover it all—the complexity of our sexual passions, the struggles of competing emotions, the infusion of aggression into our most intimate relationships, blissful surrenders, rapid couplings and ultimate, painful separations. Now listen to Beatriz as she declares:

> After Carlos' passing, tango became my royal road to healing, my way to mourn while in a tango embrace with friends. How would I have coped without the music, the lyrics, the utterly humane embrace? It would have been close to impossible to be where I am today. I know that. Dancing was an integral part of my life and it became part of my way of grieving.

Indeed, the tango becomes a primary venue for her to express not only the phantasmagorical array of feelings which accompany her healing from grief but the dance's very essence becomes an avatar of her rapidly shifting healing processes. We observe her pulling this way against certain feelings and people and then that way against the same feelings and people. Her attitudes toward past, present and future sway and dip this way and lurch that way. Her relationships with men, now as a single woman, undulate, morph and do angry battle until she accepts and rejects an altered self coming to life in an

---

2. The name adopted by the people of Buenos Aires to refer to themselves.
3. *In Strangers' Arms: The Magic of the Tango* was published by McFarland in 2011.

altered universe. And like psychoanalysis, the tango does not provide answers but immerses her in a process in which she can heal. I was mesmerized, as I assume most readers will be, by the tempestuous tempos of her mutative tango.

Furthermore, we witness her joyful assertion as a dancer:

> I am glad to learn that my grief is my own improvised dance, that I am not supposed to follow a choreography.

And the choreography she creates is replete with so many of the normal human responses to a death. She invites us to witness her irrational beliefs and temporary bursts of insanity that most mourners will recognize, like her searching for Carlos, alive and strolling blithely through town. We discover her bouts of anger, both rational and non-sensical, toward certain old friends including lapsed tango partners, and several of the medical systems she wrestled with during Carlos' illness. Intense guilt descends periodically, as when we observe her struggle with questioning her love for her husband when she is not as miserable as she thinks she should be. Incongruous self-doubt rears its ugly head in this remarkably strong, assertive and sophisticated professional woman. We see her stumble in some relationships, rejecting some and cherishing others, even in chance encounters. But her wise psychoanalyst accepts and pronounces all as normal shadings of grief. And she knows this and she is soothed.

Beatriz reminds us that grief is intricately tied up with temporality. She announces, "This afternoon I am an overlap of past and present." My mind switches to the ancient Greeks who distinguished between two types of time, *Chronos* and *Kairos*. Chronos is the stuff of objective, tick-tock time. As such her depiction of grief is replete with birthdays, anniversaries, deaths, and personal remembrances, such as the day young Beatriz and Carlos left Buenos Aires to live in the States, the day Carlos became ill, the day he died. Kairos, on the other hand, refers to our subjective, internal sense of time, a time that may or, in particular, may not coincide with objective reality. This is a kind of time where a minute can feel like an hour and a lifetime can feel like a second. This is the kind of time that can travel back and forth among present, past and future. This is a distinctively human time, determined by our guts and not by the big forces and equations of the universe such as gravity, light and entropy. And this time is embedded uniquely in each of us.

Kairos and Chronos work in tandem and sometimes dialectically to provide the context of our grieving. This idea is crucial for several reasons. If a mental health professional has a half-chance of truly helping someone who is dealing unsuccessfully with grief, the importance of our grasping both senses of time is a necessity.

Considering Chronos first, who says mourning must be finished by a year? That may be the case for many, or that might be what the priests and rabbis of ancient times were pressing for. To be human is to have your own internal clock, determined by too many variables to synthesize and make sense of. Beatriz is spot on when she compares mourning to choreography—each person creates their own. The successful mourner or clinician attempting to help the person grieving needs to accept this.

And, as Beatriz so ably gets across, grief is about the vicissitudes, the unexpected twists and turns, of Kairos. Our internal world can seem to enter a time machine whose temporal gauges are shattered, as we swing unpredictably from present to past to future to present. And if mourning is to be successful, this experience also needs to be heard, accepted and respected, again, both by the mourner and the person helping the mourner. Eventually, when mourning is successful the mourner will begin dreaming up new templates and new roads to guide their journey into a future emerging with increasing clarity from behind the mist of grief infused oblivion.

In the Epilogue, which takes place a year later, Beatriz ends with an anecdote so wickedly delightful that my trying to retell it could not come close to doing it justice. So I will leave you in suspense. You will have to read the book. But I can say her anecdote captures the essence of her recovery and underlines how this book can be of enormous help to anyone undergoing the excruciating pain of the loss of a loved one.

Neil J. Skolnick, Ph.D., is a psychologist/psychoanalyst practicing in New York City. He is a clinical associate professor at the New York University Postdoctoral Program in Psychotherapy and Psychoanalysis. His most recent book, published by Routledge in 2020, is Relational Psychoanalysis and Temporality: Time Out of Mind.

References

Dujovne, B. (2011). *In Strangers' Arms: The Magic of the Tango.* Jefferson, NC: McFarland.

Kübler-Ross, E. (1969). *On Death and Dying.* New York: Routledge.

Romero, S. "Do Argentinians Need Therapy? Pull Up a Couch." *New York Times* (2020, March 25).

Introduction

This book is about a woman in grief.

She is bewildered by the death of her husband, her lifelong companion who was bigger than life itself. She is no longer sure who she is, reduced to one half of the couple they formed for most of their lives. She has been shaken, seismically; her whole world has shifted; her place in the world has become frighteningly uncertain.

The woman is also a psychologist, an author, a dancer. She researches her home country of Argentina. She enters psychotherapy to grieve and to rebuild herself from the ashes of her loss. In the narrative which forms most of this book, you will see her as a regular woman groping through the darkness of her story. But here, outside the narrative, the psychologist has something to tell you and all the people around you who might be facing the loss of a loved one.

There is no script for grieving.

Therapy showed me that mourning is an odd and complex process. There is no road map for it. What I learned in graduate school is that people go through five emotional stages after experiencing a loss, and that these stages are assumed to follow a certain progression. It sounds very tidy. And it is very misleading.

The process of therapy I portray here offers a counterexample to most of the approaches to grief which I encountered and studied in the United States. Its only agenda was to help me with voicing the ineffable, experiencing what I did not know I had inside me, and reliving horrors that were trapped in my body. My sessions provided me with a nonjudgmental environment where every emotion, without exception, was welcomed and even elicited. And it went further: with my therapist's skills and my commitment to search for my inner truth, we unveiled unconscious conflicts when they impeded my progress. I improvised my own dance of grief—not as a theoretical model dictates, but as I discovered it, and as many bereaved patients discover in their own ways once they find the same enabling environment and the guidance of a helpful therapist.

In her 1969 book *On Death and Dying,* the Swiss-American psychiatrist Elisabeth Kübler-Ross delineated the now famous theory of "five stages of grief." Her work with terminally ill patients, conducted at North American institutions, gestated this description of an emotional development of coping patterns—*in the dying person.* Somehow these stages became widely used as a road map for the treatment *of the grieving person.* Soon taught as training at educational institutions, this stage-model of grief was also quickly adopted by our popular culture and universalized by its repetition across swarms of self-help books. Although scholars, including Kübler-Ross herself, have questioned the legitimacy of this sequential stage-model of mourning, our culture cannot quite let go of the classically clean picture it offers. It fits our cultural preferences, like a glove fits the hand. Our culture does not feel comfortable with "messy" emotions. Organizing the messy phenomena of bereavement into neat little boxes is just too seductive and too convenient.

Accepted therapies are the result of a particular cultural background. Mainstream approaches that thrive in our American culture focus on the correction of faulty cognitions; other methodologies treat behaviors that can be observed and quantified. Parallel to these mainstream paradigms lies the humanistic approach, an umbrella term that covers a range of modalities practiced by professionals with diverse degrees. These therapies navigate conscious experiences. Psychoanalytic psychotherapy, less known and less used in the States, is a form of in-depth talking therapy that aims to bring unconscious emotions and conflicts to awareness.

Trying to choose a therapist is difficult in this culture, where we cannot ask friends or relatives for recommendations, since most people do not have the experience of being in therapy. When we moved to Portland, at the very peak of my husband's lengthy illness, I felt as lost as most regular people do; I didn't know where to turn to find in-depth therapy and the best therapist for me. At that time, with stress at a maximum and time of the essence, I followed the shortest route to find one—I asked my medical doctor. Like most physicians in this culture, she didn't know any therapists personally. She handed me the card of someone who had a Ph.D. in counseling after her name: it said she "specialized in grief."

I attended several sessions. We had a good rapport, but I found her cognitive approach unsuited to me: she elicited my thoughts rather than my emotions. Her treatment was offering me nothing more than I could already see in myself. In the weeks following my husband's death, I skimmed the opening chapters of several self-help books written with dry words. I put them back on the shelf; they were written for the brain merely.

In the United States, two cultural leitmotifs discourage people from pursuing psychotherapy: the glorification of positive thinking and the pervasive ideal of the self-made person. The "negative" emotions of the grieving person do not find expression when people around them are solely comfortable with positive emotions. The image of the self-made entrepreneur, a term coined in the 1800s to describe those whose success depended on themselves—which is to say on their capital and their initiative—has created an expectation that one has to heal without outside help.

I did not want to be treated by a "specialist in grief." Nor did I want to be taught "how to cope." My world had collapsed. I felt like a stranger to myself. I wanted an empathic generalist who could address the depths of raw emotion residing in my heart and my viscera. I needed expert guidance for performing the creative act of reinventing myself.

I had studied the major therapeutic modalities at academic institutions here and in Argentina: Sigmund Freud and his followers for five years; behavior therapy for two years; humanistic psychology for three years. I had a broader training in psychology than the American cultural mainstream could steer me toward, and I decided to use it.

I escaped our cultural "do it yourself" and "think positively" ideology. I went to my birth city in that other America, that continent in the south—a city where most therapists are trained in psychoanalytic psychology and in the workings of the unconscious. I placed myself in a culture where it is natural to seek therapy for the grieving person and for whole families, including children—and not after the moment of crisis, but before intractable conditions develop.

In our first-world country, our minds are not generally open to seeking therapy when a major loss occurs; it doesn't cross people's minds to seek help after a major loss. It doesn't seem like a realistic option to us until well after recalcitrant symptoms have already developed either in our bodies or our minds as a result of unresolved bereavement issues—that is, when it is too late. And once it is too late, we often receive prescriptions for psycho-chemicals instead of human help.

The monumental dislocation we experience after the earthquake of losing someone is an identity changer. It wipes out our worldview and leaves us disoriented in ways we cannot prepare for. To emerge from the ashes of loss with the ability to embrace life and to tap into our creative resources requires expert assistance from therapists who have an optimal emotional distance from us. I recommend therapy for significant losses—without exception. Why wait until the house is on fire to buy a smoke alarm? Why shoulder your burdens alone and walk the rest of your life under their weight?

My hope is that the narrative in this book can offer empathic resonance and new insights, and can open new paths to individuals grieving or facing the oncoming death of loved ones. At one point, I thought I wasn't suffering enough—a thought which deserves to cross no person's mind. *There is no script for everyone.* Inside you there is your own road map which you may not be able to read on your own. Therapy can give you that other set of eyes, that other set of ears, that other human contact—the most natural way to find ourselves and our sense of wholeness.

Note on the Psychoanalytic Sessions

The sessions depicted in this narrative have been reconstructed from the notes I took after they occurred. Some portrayals represent complete sessions while others are segments recounting how specific quandaries were resolved. The sessions appear in the order in which they occurred but they do not represent a complete sequence: not every session I experienced is shown in this book. They are meant to offer the reader a semblance of what six months of psychoanalytic therapy can address. This form of therapy fosters an expression of what spontaneously comes to the client's mind, which is circular rather than linear in nature, so for the sake of clarity, I have edited them to approach a more linear format.

1

Flying from Autumn to Spring

The city where I will be landing within the hour has enamored me for my whole life. And not just because I was born and raised there, in Buenos Aires, the Paris of South America. I treasure the warmth that oozes from her pores. I love her people's way of being in the world. There I can relate to family, to friends, even to strangers, in ways I never practice in the States. I can greet them with hugs and kisses. I can touch the arms and hold the hands of those I speak with. I can receive the same simple, human touch from them. I can look people straight in the eye—a custom so normal in this land. Knowing the world will not explode when people touch each other during casual conversation makes me ecstatic. At my back stands a cold autumn in Portland, but under the clouds below me lies the great port city of South America, where it is the stirring start of spring.

I love Buenos Aires for the emotions she brings up in me. There is nothing like the sweet high of interconnection she offers, with her humans mingling outdoors in her innumerable streets and her manicured green parks, with the nostalgias of her tango music and her French architecture, with her bookstores more numerous than anywhere else in the world, with her overflowing cornucopia of cafés and theaters where the milk and wheat of the interior meet the international sphere of a buzzing media planet. I even like her perfidious sidewalks, where I have landed on my face too many times and once even fractured my wrists.

I know her inside and out. I feel eager to dive into the high energy that makes my heart beat faster and faster. I look forward to the surprises she harbors for me. She is inexhaustible in her arts, her lectures, her workshops; no one can explore all forty-five of her uniquely different districts; no one can fully take her in. Riding her subways or in her cabs is a guaranteed adventure.

As the plane draws closer, I feel myself ready for them.

I need to embark upon them.

I have my reasons.

Using your miles for an upgrade to business class has its advantages. It is quiet. It seems so far removed from the action of the main cabin. The lights are kept dimmed, inviting sleep and creating a hazy special effects atmosphere. Everything looks white here. The seats look too short for a fully reclined person, with the legs sliding under and alongside the seat in front. They look like tubs with white rounded headboards, isolating all the passengers from their neighbors. Short-walled white cribs, for little baby people, covered up to their heads with impeccably white ironed blankets and pillowcases. Business class feels more and more like an emergency hospital incubator than a commercial airliner for adults. When I dozed off earlier, I conjured up a nurse who descended from heaven to console my broken heart while I sleep. The real nurses were bringing me wine and spirits to soothe my nerves. I skipped dinner because I expected it would taste bland despite the hushed ambience, the little white tablecloth, and the real china. These days I only eat minimal bites, and I save my appetite for tidbits of real quality.

As we begin our descent, we are four hours ahead of where my trip started in the Pacific Northwest. The nap I took will do me some good: to miss even half a day is to give up too much. My visits to Buenos Aires always feel too brief, even the longest ones that lasted several months for research. My acquaintances in the States, where I have lived most of my adult life, invariably ask me: "Are you going to visit friends?" They look rather incredulous when I tell them, "I don't have many friends in Buenos Aires; the city is my friend." My stateside friends assumed I boarded this plane to head south and dance tango, as I have regularly done in recent years. No. Dancing is the last thing on my mind at the moment.

1. Flying from Autumn to Spring

This year I am going for more than the city, and for more than her tango.

I am making this journey to bring her my broken heart after the colossal loss of my lifelong husband. "Husband" is such an inadequate term to describe him. He was bigger than life itself: my favorite person, my cheerleader, my cocoon, my protector, my advisor, my friend. He was the first doctor I consulted when I did not feel well. People who met us together could see right away that he looked at me with a glow in his eyes. We were two strong individuals seamlessly intertwined even when we were apart.

I started grieving Carlos before he died, during the three difficult years that transpired between his cancer diagnosis and the end. We had plenty of time to navigate our way through terribly sad moments as well as some very happy times. We talked and we talked, processing what we were both going through. Our favorite conversations were about how our dreams came true because of our marriage, how special our relationship had always been, how proud we were of the family we formed. And how we were not ready for the end of our marriage. And how we had been counting on many more years together.

Promise me you won't stay sad after I die.

That's what he whispered to me, on our last night together. We were both depleted from fighting off sleep in our struggle to steal more time with each other. With strength I didn't have anymore and eyelids growing heavy, I was stretching my arm to turn out the lights when his words took me by surprise. They were totally in line with the selfless human being he was.

Don't forget to do what makes you happy.
If you do, I can be happy too.

He also said *Ojo,* which in Spanish means "be cautious." I asked what I should be cautious about. He hesitated to complete his sentence and moved his hand implying: "Erase what I began to say." He probably did not want to alarm me.

Ten hours later, he was gone.

My husband's words opened up life's possibilities to me. Not a day has passed without me feeling guided by them, protected by them.

17

They cheer me up. They are looking after me. They follow me—but I don't always know how to follow them. No matter how much we grieved together before he died, no matter how much I have grieved since his death, I know that my heart has more healing it needs to do. There is grieving ahead of me yet.

Now I am a single person, a widow. In that vast city emerging from the clouds below, I won't be judged if I venture outside my comfort zone and don't handle it well. I will have the chance to be what I am, to go through what I am going through. I will feel freer to be myself down there, in Buenos Aires.

Psychotherapy will help me, piece by piece, to reconstruct my present life and to find out who I am now. I do not want to walk through this passage of life blind to my unconscious. I want to know the all of me, so I can move forward—centered, maintaining my own balance. I want to plant the seeds of my new identity, as a person living on my own.

Precisely because this is a major undertaking, I have chosen a psychoanalyst to help me through this process with the in-depth approach that characterizes his technique. Dr. Novelli was my husband's psychoanalyst recently; I pat myself on the back for having scheduled regular appointments with him now, the first one just a few days after my arrival. During our last trip here together, Carlos set up a joint session for the two of us. Did he plan to have me meet his therapist, in case I needed one myself in the near future?

Why did I choose psychoanalysis? I am a psychologist trained in both countries. Among all the methods of therapy, I prefer the psychoanalytic one that brings unconscious emotions and conflicts into present awareness, as opposed to the cognitive or behavioral methods that navigate consciousness, which are used by most therapists in the States. Self-help books that offer advice to the grieving person do not resonate with me very much. Both of those tools scratch the surface— they don't reach down to the level of raw emotion. Sure, many people in the United States think they should be grieving by themselves. Chances are they could do it faster and better with the assistance of psychotherapy.

The professional in me found Dr. Novelli alert and humane during our single joint session. "If I need a therapist," I told Carlos, "he will be the one." He greeted us warmly with a kiss on the cheek, which is not strange in Buenos Aires. And he knows very well who Carlos was, and what he meant to everyone around him. He won't assume I am idealizing him just because he died.

Buenos Aires is the place for me to do this. Psychoanalysis is widely accepted here. Argentines turn to the type of psychotherapy founded by Sigmund Freud both to foster personal growth and to treat emotional suffering. Regular folks use it for themselves and their families without hesitation. We are familiar with its benefits. The practice became embedded in Argentine culture from the time of Freud's initial publications; in the 1890s, before Freud's work was even translated into Spanish, medical doctors in Argentina were discussing his publications in French. Psychoanalysis became so ingrained in the culture that even talk on the street includes terms like the subconscious, free association, ambivalence, neurosis, Oedipus complex. When there is a death in the family here, locals go to therapy and take their children along. They don't label themselves weak or mentally ill for seeking help. They don't hide it; on the contrary, they think it is the smart thing to do. Friends feel free to discuss their sessions over a cup of coffee. Comparatively speaking, most forms of psychoanalytic psychotherapy in the United States have become stigmatized. Psychology has been embraced in the objectively oriented culture of the United States more for its attention to behavior modification than for its value helping us navigate introspection and the secret workings of the unconscious.

So I am planning to do what most people do in Buenos Aires—go to therapy before my movement forward gets arrested, and before my troubles have a chance to become severe health problems. I want to make sure my health and independence do not get blocked by unresolved guilt, depression, or any of the many other life problems related to unresolved bereavement.

I have gone through the experience of forging a new identity once before. I did it when Carlos and I emigrated from Buenos Aires to Chicago in the late 1960s. It was easier then because Carlos and I had each other, and together we figured out how to exist in our new city, in our new country, speaking a different language, adopting a culture that was orderly, predictable, and safe. The new stability didn't have the old salt and pepper of Buenos Aires. Carlos did not miss that as much as I did. The opportunity to pursue his passion for medical research in the United States gave him a lifelong supply of excitement.

So here I am. After decades together, I have to figure out who I am—cut away from Carlos. We were inseparable before, but now I am feeling like one very separable individual.

Reality check. The stewardess' voice announces flight 110 from Atlanta is about to end—the plane will touch down in just a few minutes. Soon I will set foot on the land which I hope will get me shaken up even more than I already am, so that all my pieces can fall apart and I can arrange them into a new form.

The landing itself must have gone smoothly, because I look up from the distraction of my ruminations to see my fellow passengers standing with their belongings, in a stationary line, waiting to proceed down the aisle. There is excitement ahead of me but I am not used to traveling alone. My throat tightens. A certain apprehension, a feeling of something missing, is trying to pull me down. Exactly at this moment of exiting the plane, Carlos would urge me to move faster and beat the crowds at customs. This time I lag a bit behind my fellow business class group. When I finally manage to disembark with them, I am the last one. Who cares?

Deplaning with hand luggage and descending into the labyrinth of walkways, turns, mechanical stairs, and elevators keeps me busy with externals. As I drift up to the customs counter with both passports in hand, my heart pounds at feeling divided in half—no other experience puts me face to face with being a citizen of two nations yet belonging to neither of them entirely. I always look forward to a greeting from the customs officer. Being warmly received in the land I abandoned in my youth feels, on some level, like being forgiven. Speaking without the foreign accent that brands my English is a relief and a welcome sense of freedom—I feel congruent again.

Once I'm approved to enter Argentina, my first challenge is approaching the luggage carousel where Carlos used to take charge. I study the porters in the area and hire a twenty-something named Pedro, expecting him to be more trustworthy than the older, more streetwise porters. Carlos taught me that generosity with tips pays off:

it can get you out of the airport faster and escorted safely to a taxi. I let shy Pedro know the tip he will receive when we are done. He handles passing through security without my having to deal with opening and closing suitcases.

As we begin to tackle this final section of the airport, a new feeling of vulnerability takes me by surprise. "Carlos, where are you? I wish I could talk with you about feeling *sola* from you—no one else would understand this." He alone knew how much Buenos Aires' *Ezeiza* airport distresses me—it has been the scene of so many separations. The night Carlos and I emigrated to the States, I was clutching a wool-lined leather coat to fend off the Chicago winters. He held that coat for me while I hugged my parents. Guilt struck me fiercely; I was their only child. Only Carlos knew the trauma I felt when I said goodbye to them here, especially to my dad. I was afraid they were going to die of sheer sadness. It was a hard moment for Carlos too; he felt a deep love for my parents and was struggling with his own guilt about splitting up the family. At that moment my body registered emotions that were to follow me for decades. Every time I saw an older man sadly embracing a young woman at any airport, the trauma of my own separation got stirred up, and I would weep uncontrollably. Diligently, Carlos and our daughter Vera would distract me from any father-daughter scene before I could notice it, redirecting my attention elsewhere with whatever excuse they could make up in the moment.

At the precise instant we boarded the departing plane for Chicago, everything in me changed. I walked down the long aisle having lost something that had to do with who I was. I was giving up something, and it was a scary change. But the loss I felt was also a moment that presaged my new life with Carlos, the beginning of a time when we would have each other *forever*. We were out on the edge of our future and striding forward, and the possibility of death was no worry to us then.

My flashbacks vanish when Pedro and I arrive at the last section of the airport, the lobby that opens to the world outside. Gentle Pedro's attentive eyes save me from being paranoid about my luggage—I just need to hold my purse close to my body to discourage thieves. And to relax, I need to relax. With Pedro I won't be fending off characters who accost me for tips after the imaginary jobs they invented just for me.

"Don't Be Sad When I'm Gone"

Boisterous locals shout the names of their relatives who are arriving from abroad. It comforts me that somebody familiar will be here to greet me. Last February, a dear old friend from graduate school sent me his customary good wishes for my birthday. He knew Carlos, and we had resumed contact in recent years. With my thank-you letter, I included the eulogy I had written for Carlos. He responded immediately:

> *Dear Bea. Thank you for sending me your "Eulogy for Carlos." I wish to accompany you with my embrace and my heart. I have always known the feelings you had, and still have, for Carlos. I feel profound sadness.*
> *Count on me.*
> *Count on me.*
> *Gustavo*

A month before this trip, I told him it was hard to imagine arriving without Carlos, and without my now deceased friend Celina meeting me at the airport, as she had done throughout the years. "Could I count on you to pick me up at the airport?" I felt glad that he said yes. Also a bit concerned. I remembered a dark side of him; he used to get very upset sometimes.

Spotting Gustavo in the lobby near the entrance, I raise my arm with a wave, smile to him, and say to myself, as in disbelief: "He *is* here!" Does my unconscious know something I have forgotten? Was Gustavo a person capable of changing his mind and not showing up? "Stay in the present, Beatriz," I advise myself. Warmed by our re-encounter after more than a year, and embracing with gusto—the Buenos Aires way—I tip the faithful Pedro before my friend and I stop at a nearby breakfast counter for a much-needed macchiato with crisp *medialunas* taken right out of the oven. Then we head to the car that will convey me and my luggage to the rented apartment which will be my temporary home for an unknown period of time. In a short forty minutes through the highways and the city streets, we pull up in front of my destination.

Once inside, I scan the familiar apartment. Carlos and I stayed here for two consecutive years. I enjoy its luminosity, the whiteness of its walls, the minimalistic décor, the spaciousness. I envision its ninety square meters spotted with bouquets of flowers for small touches of warmth. We set down my baggage.

It is getting close to lunchtime. Gustavo and I walk under the shade of the *tipas*, the trees that line the sidewalks of Buenos Aires—I realize how much I miss these trees in the States; they give Buenos Aires as much personality as its French architecture. We enjoy lunch together at Las Delicias, a nearby restaurant on Quintana, near Callao. I don't feel this is a good time to talk about Carlos' death, so I keep that hell to myself. In response to my questions, Gustavo says he has had serious health issues, but he prefers to postpone talking about it until a later time. I feel secretly glad that he is keeping his hell to himself. There are times to refrain and there are times to share one's hell. After a brief walk around the neighborhood, we bid each other goodbye with a hug, and he leaves. Turning back twice, he moves his lips, saying:

Count on me.
Count on me.

Can I count on him? Why am I even asking this question? And who am I asking?

2

Not Just
Another Husband

Impossible strategies are all I can think of this morning, as I anticipate my first appointment with Dr. Novelli. Persistent questions keep buzzing around my mind: How can I convey to him the gargantuan size of my loss? Shall I talk about our marriage, or the ups and downs of Carlos' terminal illness? Or about how I haven't been able to cry for months now? Nothing will fit into a fifty-minute session.

Why do I keep doing this mental exercise? As futile as it is, it binds my anxiety about the unknowns that will come up in therapy. I know Dr. Novelli will expect me to say what comes to my mind spontaneously, without me bringing prefabricated topics to our sessions. So why am I obsessing over contradictions?

I see my paradox—I have grown anxious about starting the therapy, which I wanted for so long. I forgive myself for being in angst on account of my loss. I can't pretend I am the same person. I can't pretend I don't have a strange feeling about myself. *My self* has changed, from the moment Carlos died. Whether I accept this or not, it has. Right now, I am a self in mourning. A self warped and distorted by grief. I also forgive myself for my angst as I know therapy will be hard at times: re-experiencing traumatic moments is part of it. I also look forward to acknowledging the difficult states I have undergone since my life-changing trauma.

I continue going in circles, asking more questions: How long will it take Dr. Novelli to grasp that Carlos was not just *any other husband?* For this, I have an answer: He will know it immediately if he reads the eulogy for Carlos. This scenario sends me on a mission: I print the pages, roll them, secure them with a rubber band, and slip the roll into my purse.

Almost ready to leave, I pause to scrutinize my Spartan apartment with its ten-foot ceilings and its recently painted white walls. I am feeling Carlos' presence strongly. He is here, in the bouquets of multicolor freesias I positioned around the living room. He used to buy them from street florists and arrive home excited to show me their colors and their aromas as we unwrapped them.

He was the flower-lover and the flower-provider of our household. This year I am the buyer and the lover of flowers—without him.

After my brief connection with Carlos through the flowers, I feel calmer about starting therapy. More than calmer—I feel relieved about the struggle of grieving by myself and practically with no support. For all of its oddness, I have been waiting for this day since Carlos left. I am ready to meet it face to face.

It's time for breakfast.

Dos Escudos, my neighborhood *panadería* (bakery), is a seventy-year-old establishment whose unique breads and fabulous desserts attract customers from all corners of Buenos Aires. It has a cozy café attached to it, patronized by locals and a few informed tourists who heard this is the best place to start the day with a genuine *porteña* experience (that is, one relating to the port city Buenos Aires). Luckily, it is just one block away from my apartment, and some days I come here more than once. Over the past nine years its small, artsy ambiance and its honestly delicious offerings have grown on me. It grows on people who come here hoping to find a table for more than a momentary experience. Like me, they like to hang out here soaking in the good vibes of the place. Typically I read the newspaper, work on my laptop, and let my mind drift while sipping my favorite macchiatos. I am now sipping a large one with a mountaintop of foam, smiling as my finger traces the mustache of milk foam—and feeling in no hurry to wipe it off.

And my writing? I haven't been able to write for two years. I need to find my writing ways again; right after arriving here, I committed to presenting a paper at the National Academy of Tango in November. I agreed to do it under the assumption that I would soon feel less possessed by Carlos' loss, with therapy liberating energies that I could devote to this work.

I feel tight as I try to contain the devastating memories I will have to start feeling anew during my session this afternoon.

During my four-block walk to therapy, my skin basks in the balmy September breeze. This is a perfect seventy-five-degree afternoon. Not taking it for granted, I walk along Avenida Alvear in an abundance of light, and along the three blocks between Montevideo and Callao I pass the "must-see" architecture of the tourist guides—the Apostolic Nunciatura, the Palacio Duhau, a Tudor Revival building, and numerous demi-palaces erected in the early 1900s.

In the last few steps before I reach Dr. Novelli's building, my U.S. friends come to mind. They used to ask me if therapists seek help from other therapists. I always responded affirmatively, adding, "We cannot be objective about ourselves." The patient's seat is not only familiar to me but also a privilege that, like other therapists in this city, I value enormously.

I ring Dr. Novelli's intercom exactly at 4:00 to respect the usual buffer of time that prevents collision with the patient exiting at 3:50. When his voice invites me to come in, I hear a click as the lock disables. A little push and I am standing inside a sparely furnished lobby, where the doorman sits. I wish him a good afternoon, and he asks where I am heading. I tell him, and he shows me which of the two elevators will take me to Dr. Novelli's office.

During the short ride up, it strikes me that most therapists in Buenos Aires have no waiting room; the cost of land may make it prohibitive. What a pity. Waiting rooms are ideal transitional zones between the outer street noise and the silence inside therapy rooms; they invite the patient to begin an introspective journey. Well, the elevator will have to do.

His office on the third floor has no receptionist—I ring the bell myself. Dr. Novelli, a tall man in his late sixties or early seventies, opens the door and greets me with a smile: *"Hola,* Beatriz. *Adelante."*

Many professionals, including doctors, greet their clients or patients with a kiss on the cheek. It is totally normal in this culture—

but I am not sure about therapists. At my initiative, we shake hands. I say nothing while scanning the office to choose a seat. There are two chairs, one beside his own and another across from it, and there is also a green sofa for three people facing his armchair. I can see treetops and blue skies outside a window on the left. I know that small talk doesn't have a place in psychoanalytic therapy sessions, so I talk to myself in silence; the chair with a straight back must be for patients with back problems. What I really crave is the analytic couch—in old times it was called the Victorian fainting couch—but I can't have it because it is reserved for long-term patients embarking on prolonged personality changes. During my practicing years, I felt attached to the purple corduroy couch I had made for patients in my office. When I moved to Portland, I sadly let it go—I still miss it. Today my mind seems to be trained on what I miss.

The moss green sofa for three people calls me. It is large enough to contain the pieces of the broken self that I am bringing for healing. I want to honor *my self in grief* while I recover my normal self, so I can feel whole again. I cozy up in the couch, between the armrest and the back, try it for comfort—like I would try a pair of shoes. It holds me softly and firmly.

There is no desk between us, which suits me well; it signals that Dr. Novelli is not an old-guard type of therapist. I get the same impression from his casual attire—blue jeans and shirt. Now we are facing one another and our gazes meet. I envision getting attached to his blue eyes; they radiate goodness—they remind me of Carlos' smiling eyes.

This is a good beginning. I feel at home in this new space, with this casual looking therapist, seated across him with no barriers in between.

"I've been here in Buenos Aires for just two days. But already I am feeling very different."

"What's different here?" Dr. Novelli asks me.

"Buenos Aires changes my tempo to *presto*. It was *adagio* in Portland. In fact, you could say I feel a bit agitated. We use the word 'wired' in English to describe this feeling." Dr. Novelli smiles as I try to find a translation into Spanish and can't think of one. "I feel more agitated than active, and can't sustain my old inner peace for longer than brief moments."

I tell him I came to the session with a mission: "I would like you to read Carlos' eulogy."

I search for the typed pages in my oversized purse and, mustering courage, I say, almost inaudibly, as if I were doing something wrong: "Here."

I hold the rolled paper out to him.

"It will be best if you read it out loud," Dr. Novelli says.

I look at him in silence and get immediately distracted by my own unusual posture: my forearms are crossed on my upper chest with my hands pressing down at the base of my throat. I don't remember being in such a position ever before. No willful intention choreographed it. It surprises me. My body is communicating something going on right now. I feel activity and noise inside my chest, a cauldron, a fight. Shielded by my crossed arms, I become tearful and contrarian. My cheeks are wet with tears.

"I don't want to read the eulogy," I say. "At the memorial last February, I had to read short paragraphs, a little at a time, and stop. I delivered it reading and stopping because I could not control my sobbing." I remember feeling like a disorganized mess inside my winter-white coat on that day. My nose would not stop running. No amount of tissues was enough. Tears are rolling down my cheeks, I need a tissue right now, but I keep on talking.

"I won't read the eulogy because I don't want to cry," I say in tears to Dr. Novelli. "I have been unable to cry for months, all the while wishing my tears would flow again. My dry eyes have been worrying me, but I don't want to read the eulogy now, and I don't want to cry." I wipe my eyes with the tips of my fingers.

Dr. Novelli gets up, walks a few steps to his desk, and looks inside a drawer. He comes to my sofa corner and offers me a sachet of tissues. His hand passing the pouch to my hand, it feels old fashioned and nice. It's more personal than taking a tissue from a box in a therapist's office in the States. We take such pride in efficiency and sanitization without realizing we lose personal contact in the process in our American culture.

"Here, Beatriz. You may use them."

He says I can have the whole sachet, when he sees my attempts to pull one tissue out of the bunch. Now, with several in my hand, I find refuge in a sobbing silence I wish to nurse for a moment. The analytic therapist in me gives Dr. Novelli a high grade for impeccable technique. I would not have read anything a patient handed me either. Pep talk: I tell myself to read the eulogy and see what happens. More pep talk: This could be a golden opportunity to open my chest and get shaken up, precisely the point of this therapy.

I begin.

Eulogy for Carlos Dujovne, my husband.
Friends,
Thank you for your company tonight.

I stop. Reading this brief beginning feels awkward. The eulogy was written for an audience. Not for someone sitting close to me. I must switch to telling, and see how it goes. The reading might distance me from Dr. Novelli—I don't want that.

"Dr. Novelli, instead of reading, I would rather tell you some details." I look up to see his reaction. He makes a gesture meaning "go ahead."

"Carlos suffered from pain since his cancer was diagnosed and surgically removed in early 2015. He sustained his hope, from that time until November 13, 2017, to be exact. On that day, he was diagnosed with the worst kind, the most painful kind of metastasis and was given one month to live. Four weeks. Can you imagine how surreal this was? Carlos, who was a Protector with a capital P, could do nothing to protect himself from such a death sentence in such a short time. And I couldn't protect him either."

I feel attacked by pangs of pain remembering that day. The tension in my body requires action; I stretch my legs away from the sofa and bring them back. I do it two or three times. Could Dr. Novelli be feeling the shock I am feeling?

"This was the shock we were under when I read the eulogy in Portland," I say. "The shock of caring for him and grieving his death at the same time. It was too sudden—too much." Looking back from my now debilitated *self in grief,* I don't know how I did it. I can hardly remember that until Carlos' last moment on this earth I was my usual strong self, organized and fully in charge. And when I wasn't, I would regain my strength through Carlos' words of love. No matter how weakened he felt, he always knew how to show his love and make me feel better. Supporting me was second nature to him.

I am glancing at the eulogy that is resting on my lap. Feeling I can only continue by anchoring myself in the written text, I proceed to read it, paraphrasing a little, to Dr. Novelli.

"I saw Carlos as a giant human being."

"Writing this eulogy was my way of being with him longer, and of honoring his uniqueness as a man—a uniqueness I could sometimes take for granted."

Since the next paragraph is about how we met back then, I could tell it in my own words without crying. So I look up and talk.

"You see, Carlos and I met after we finished our graduate studies, his in medicine and mine in psychology. I had lived in just two neighborhoods of Buenos Aires all my life, until we got married. His family had moved from Chaco, a state in northern Argentina where he was born, to Buenos Aires, where they lived in two different neighborhoods. He had moved around more than I had—geographically speaking. Also he had moved further than I had in the scope of his thinking—he saw himself as a person in the wide world.

"When we began to date, he shared his ideals about countries with no boundaries and no armies, and people of different religions coexisting in peace. I had not yet considered such large issues; I was still thinking about myself. The future I had envisioned was local. He opened my mind to a complex world beyond Argentina. As our relationship developed, he used to beam when sharing dreams with me. His cherished one was having ten children of different races around our future dining table."

I smile at this idea and add, "It would have been a handful of cute kiddies, and chaos for an introverted person like me, who had grown up in a small family of three." I pause; Dr. Novelli smiles and encourages me on.

"I had to face the fact that Carlos' future was not local, that the world was his future playground. His professional dream was moving to the United States to engage in academic medical research. He was passionate about that."

I recall being eighteen when he first mentioned migration. I shivered. But I soon understood he needed to be free to fly away and fulfill his destiny. We could marry and go together—his preferred choice. Or I could stay longer in Buenos Aires and join him later, when I was more prepared. We were sure our relationship was rock solid and would be healthy no matter where we lived. Despite my initial trembling about separating from my parents, I decided to go with him. We decided to emigrate. He would later agree with me that this was the only non-negotiable issue in our lifelong story.

I look from my lap back into the gentle eyes of Dr. Novelli.

"How could I have trembled about joining him in a life adventure? I used to say I married him because he was the most mature man I had ever known, but his heart and liberal ideas made a big impression on me. His basically happy disposition attracted me like a magnet. He was a storyteller. It was fun being around him. His smile magically erased my proclivity to worry. His strong sense of family assured me he would always have my back. For some reason it was important to me, trusting he would not disconnect from me. My Carlos, it was so easy to love him and to be loved by him!"

I need to stall; a big cry coming up is about to overtake me. I look for a distraction to minimize and divert the tears. I scan the office and discover an extension to the right that I had not seen before. Through the door, ajar, there are dark wooden shelves with books lining two walls. Carlos and I had put together so many shelves during our many moves within the States. Will Carlos become the measure of all things? I take a deep breath; look at the skies out the window on the left; let myself feel lost missing him to love. Shrugging my shoulders helps bring me back—I dab at my eyes and continue.

"Decades later the world did become his playground as he traveled within Europe and the Orient, spreading his research findings. His early passion never abated. He published his last article a year before his death, well into retirement."

Dr. Novelli is observing me with absolute concentration. I need to pause a moment. I feel grateful for the nourishment of therapy, for the irreplaceable space of freedom and safety it is offering me. How do people live without being attentively listened to, without being known—nowadays people have stopped listening to each other. After musing for a couple minutes, I again lift the eulogy and read.

"Don't Be Sad When I'm Gone"

"It was he—not I—who brought into our relationship the skills one gets growing up in an extended and closely knit family. He loved his Turkish, Polish, and Russian grandparents, and his many aunts, uncles, and cousins. As an only child, I was impressed with his large family, his many family stories and celebrations. His love for his mother Aida knew no bounds; I was in awe when he spoke about her with such emotion."

In my musings I get lost remembering that during our dating, I would tell myself that if he loved his mother so dearly, he would love me with the same devotion. Responding to my silence, Dr. Novelli's voice captures my attention.

"Beatriz, you seem to have a lot more to say."

"Yes, I do, and I am getting ready to read the next paragraph because I'd like you to hear it as I wrote it for his memorial. It is about fun memories."

Dr. Novelli nods to express his interest in hearing more.

"The Beatriz who had lived in a single zip code, and the Carlos who had roamed the world in his imagination, boarded the plane that would carry them to the United States. Later, when Carlos was doing his post-medical training at Mount Sinai Hospital in Chicago, we lived in a diverse place called Kling Residence, a multilingual apartment building for recently arrived immigrant doctors—residents, interns, and their families. Each family spoke its maternal language at home; in the playground, the mothers interacted in broken English.

"This was our first home; life was good, even our Formica furniture which I polished with Pledge before taking pictures to send to my beloved grandmother seemed beautiful. We started our family during our second year after arrival. Life gave us one daughter. Our joy was immeasurable. For years Carlos kept saying, 'It was the happiest day of my life.' With Vera, our new love at home, Carlos never failed to be present as a father and a husband, regardless of the time his academic duties took. Those were the days when research was done by hand and foot, going to the National Library of Medicine and spending the day there, looking up references in card catalogues. When Vera was just three years old, and he published his first research article in the *New England Journal of Medicine,* he continued to be a present dad. His career had a glorious start. Our dreams of family and work were becoming reality."

I raise my eyes from the text, engage Dr. Novelli's eyes, and tell him: "This was such a hard-working and happy time for us. Around thirty-five years later, Vera initiated us into our next stage of life, making us grandparents. She gave birth to three children that became the center of Carlos' life. They became his joy and pride. He fell in love with them. Literally. He could not wait to see them, to tell them how wonderful they are, and to affirm their evolving individualities."

My eyes swell when I glance at what is coming up next in the eulogy. The bundle of tissues I had been using to dry my eyes is now a wet ball. After a few minutes, I push ahead and read some more from the printout:

"We enjoyed each other's company throughout the years; we easily smiled when our eyes met because we liked each other. Never did we go to bed angry. We gave each other a long bear hug in the morning. People frequently asked us what the secret of our marriage was. I responded it was our knack for negotiating differences. Carlos joked saying it was because he did all I wanted him to do—with a big smile on his face.

"He was not possessive. He was not jealous. He encouraged me to pursue many interests, as he did himself. Whether I was performing a dance showcase or lecturing, Carlos was always in the audience. Last October at our Portland Tango Festival, he could hardly walk, and despite his disabling fatigue, he insisted on attending my presentation on the artistic culture surrounding the origins of tango. He did not want to miss it. I call this "support" with capital letters."

Remembering how weak he was at that tango festival brings tears to my eyes. Words blur on the page. I tell Dr. Novelli that I am having a hard time collecting myself. With a hand gesture he signals and tells me, "Take your time, Beatriz." After some moments, I put the eulogy down and say:

"Dr. Novelli: When I talk about Carlos' suffering I get extremely sad and I cry. When I talk about his goodness, I feel emotional in a good way and I cry. I seem to cry in empathy and in gratitude."

"That's the way it is, Beatriz."

I pause to look at his face. The attention he is giving me today is precious. I shift in my corner of the couch, clear my throat, and resume reading with some trepidation:

"Throughout the years, I recognized that Carlos was a selfless person with those in his inner circle. I can't say that about myself or anyone else I know well. He taught me, by example, that it is a generally a good idea to say 'I am sorry' to loved ones, even when he was not at fault. This is a hard lesson to learn. To learn it, one has to prefer connection to war, and to forget about 'ego' … as Carlos could easily do."

I am crying about Carlos' wisdom, looking down, drying my tears. I raise my eyes and notice that Dr. Novelli's eyes are red and watery. I sense he is touched by Carlos' wisdom too. He could be admiring Carlos at this very moment, as I am. As an experienced therapist he has to know that most people cannot forget "ego" as Carlos could so easily. I am crying almost as much as I did during the February memorial service at Congregation Beth Israel in Portland. That was six months ago and half a world away. Dr. Novelli could also be sad, as Carlos' former therapist. Trying to anchor myself in his eyes, I see they are still red and tearful. After what feels like my longest pause ever, I feel ready to go on.

"Even when his health began to decline and his big warm smile became constricted by pain, he remained the gentleman he had always been, still insisting on opening doors for me, even if he had to go around to the driver's side of the car with the support of his cane. It gave him great satisfaction to do this. His sweet self was very alive and well to the very end. Although during the last several months he did not drive to bring flowers home, he still made sure we had them."

Feeling totally spent from the labor of re-experiencing these moments, I wonder if I should stop now and save the rest of my reading for next time. I change my mind and continue:

"Two weeks before his death, Carlos met our family members one by one. He told me to take care of the family. I would not be surprised if he told each of us the same thing. Carlos was a protector. That—I now realize—was the emotional maturity that attracted me to him early on."

I stand up and walk around the office trying to gather myself—I feel calmer looking at the trees through the window on the left. I am grateful for Dr. Novelli's silence today. He and I both know it is best not to ruin with words these moments of high emotional intensity.

"Carlos' natural capacity for gratitude became magnified during the last weeks of his life. He never ceased to tell me how lucky he felt being married to me. He would thank me often and profusely for my caring of him. And each time I replied that I really loved caring for him myself, that I was enjoying the togetherness of our last days and our stronger than ever mutual devotion. I was giving him back some of the magnanimity I had received from him.

"It was a privilege to be able to share the process of death with my husband. I am thankful he was sufficiently conscious and alert, and that we could have conversations as usual."

I can hardly finish this last sentence. I let the eulogy roll itself back up in my lap. I have just relived Carlos' pain, my pain. Can they be separated?

After making it through the reading, there is no room for anything else other than silence. I collect the pieces of myself spread around the corner of the couch. My body feels boneless. Reliving Carlos' suffering and his goodness has this effect on me; it wipes me out. All I want to do now is get up, hurry home, lie in bed, and sleep. Until I wake up on my own. I hold my head with both hands and close my eyes for a moment. I move my head quickly from side to side in an effort to shake the fog. I yawn. Dr. Novelli and I are still here. The window to the left still frames the sky. A dog barks. I get up and head toward the door, not sure if the session is over. And if it isn't, what difference does that make? Dr. Novelli stands at the door but instead of shaking hands, he clasps my right hand between his two hands for a moment. I know he has stayed attuned to my agony.

Once in the elevator I notice that the cauldron in my chest had been melted down into the tears I just shed. The tears I could not cry for six months, the ones I thought had abandoned me forever. Had Dr. Novelli read the eulogy, I would have avoided the first good cry I've had in six months. Therapy often has the effect of a gradual betterment, but sometimes results show immediately, like my tears flowing now, during today's session, after their season of drought.

I leave the building still in a haze. Posadas Street doesn't seem quite in focus. I stop at the corner café and ask for a grapefruit juice at the counter.

"Don't Be Sad When I'm Gone"

Still yawning, I feel my lungs craving oxygen. I head in the opposite direction of my apartment. Ahead of me, a ten-minute walk from where I am, are Thays Park and Plazoleta Juan XXIII, two green spaces adjacent to each other. When I am about halfway there, the colonial Iglesia del Pilar appears in the distance, painted in white and ochre.

By the time I reach the center of the park, it feels enlivening to yawn with gusto among the three-hundred-year-old *gomero* trees. I soothe myself stretching my arms as wide as I can, inhaling and exhaling, strolling around the manicured green, and feeling the spring air on my face. My shoes go to my purse in no time once I discover the new green grass under my feet. I close my eyes to feel the tickling of grass on my soles.

At the south end of the green space, about two hundred meters from here, artisan shops line the longest path of this park with their white canopies; they sell the goods that tourists like to buy. Watching the action from a distance is sufficient for me today.

I sit on a park bench to put my shoes on. Music from the artisans' area makes me pause and listen. A violinist is playing Astor Piazzolla's "Adios, Nonino" (Goodbye, Dad), an extremely tender piece that he composed when his father died.

When the song ends and the emphatic violin subsides, I feel more awake. I have an acute craving—for a soft bed.

3

Elusive Encounters

This morning I was working as Dr. Dujovne with my patients through Skype. Due to the four-hour time difference with the West Coast of the United States, I am leaving home later than usual, uncertain if I will be in time for breakfast at Dos Escudos.

Martín, the Middle Eastern-looking server, lets me know right away that I missed breakfast and may also miss lunch if I don't select one of the daily hot lunches—and *presto*. He dashes back with the menu and asks if I want to drink a glass of wine. Craving the macchiato I haven't yet had today, I tell him quickly: "I would like a double one, Martín, as fast as possible, and for lunch a *milanesa a caballo* (breaded beef "on horseback"—topped with two fried eggs) and *papas provenzal* (potatoes with Provençal sauce). No wine for me at noon, thank you, Martín."

I like to set my mind in drifting mode while I am sipping my double macchiato and lunch gets prepared. Now I know differently that coming here to grieve makes total sense—this trip is no vacation, and no distraction from my lingering agony. On the contrary, everything here is drenched in memories I dearly welcome. Right now, in my mind's eye, Carlos and I are sitting here, at this café, eating lunch, as we have done for nine consecutive years, interacting with the servers—three women and Martín, who all wear white kitchen headwear, identical white jacket uniforms, and their cute jeans below. Carlos and these women used to engage in a playful rapport. Martín couldn't break into the inner circle of the women taking turns catering to Carlos, as they jealously teased that his sense of humor and his compliments made their day.

Along with the macchiato and the remembrances, I am savoring last night's show at our majestic opera house, the Teatro Colón. I so missed Carlos there; he would have loved watching tenor José Diego Flores at the peak of his splendor. We shared the excitement of attending his debut in the United States around 2001, in Kansas City, where we lived at the time. I skim through the photos I took last night. They are all well composed selfies, showcasing the theater's ornate upper boxes behind me, with all their gold-leaf trim. Something puzzles me about the pictures; they show only half of my face. A little more scrolling reveals that I have been taking half-face images in Buenos Aires for two weeks.

I must mention this to Dr. Novelli. In some upcoming session, I must also mention to him that my initially warm companionship with Gustavo has turned brittle after four weeks; it may break at any time for any reason at all. This change is puzzling me. During our short good days, we were laughing so much that sometimes we laughed about how much we were laughing. Where did the relaxed Gustavo go? Staying connected is a challenge now, and it is tiring me out.

After lunch I put the photos away and go back to typing up a note about Diego Flores for my tango book's website. I lose track of time; when I look up at the clock, I realize my session will start in fifteen minutes. Promptly I pay and leave, hoping meanwhile to recover this habit of writing for a couple of hours at Dos Escudos, as I did in previous years. I need to find my writing ways again: right after arriving here, I committed to presenting a paper at the Fourth Congress of the National Academy of Tango in November, which is right around the corner. This year's theme is "The Many Languages of Tango," and I chose to submit a paper under the subheading "Dance Expressions of Tango." I made the pledge to participate under the assumption that I would soon feel less consumed by Carlos' loss, with therapy liberating the energies I could use for writing.

I hurry up to make my session.

Coming back to reality, I wonder if I will be able to find the building again. I left Dr. Novelli's card with his address at home. After walking for twelve minutes I spot Fervor from afar, which is exactly across the street from Dr. Novelli's office. Fervor was Carlos' favorite meat restaurant in the entire city—Buenos Aires can't help but wound me at every corner, pounding into my brain that I am without him, that Carlos' absence is irreversible. I tell myself not to worry—that *she* knows how to console me. *She* will spark memories inscribed in my neurons, forgotten experiences that have the potential to be activated and transmuted into fresh memories. This nearness to the roots of our life together will make that happen. Hopefully the mingling of new memories with the old ones will soothe me rather than wound me.

I walk up to my destination. The doorman is smoking outside, under the shade of one of the enormous *tipa* trees that line the streets of Buenos Aires making a green canopy. I greet him.

"Good afternoon; I am not sure which floor is Dr. Novelli's office."

"Six," he says. He has a look of obvious uncertainty.

Knowing that many Argentine men invent what they don't know, I thank him and add: "I was here last week, my intuition tells me it's on three. I will ring three first." As I do, Dr. Novelli's voice comes through the intercom: "Hello."

"It is Beatriz," I say. A click disengages the entry door. I open it and walk through the small lobby. Regular life will stay behind me once I enter the petite elevator that seems smaller than last time. Everything will be out of my mind: plans for tonight, weather, traffic, people. Moving automatically now, I exit the elevator; I walk to the left; I ring office 34. Dr. Novelli, seeming taller than last week, opens the door. My weekly introspective adventure is about to begin.

I enter this other world of quietude, empathy, understanding, and the luxury of not being judged.

Once inside, before sitting down, I give him the good news: "Last session I needed to read the eulogy to shake up my raw core. My tears brought an end to my six-month dry spell. I am feeling hopeful about keeping them flowing."

As I begin to turn my gaze inside, a leftover memory forms in my mind. I share it.

"I get anxious having dinner by myself in Buenos Aires. I don't feel that way in the United States."

"Let's see, Beatriz."

"For example, I missed Carlos at Rodi's last night."

"Don't Be Sad When I'm Gone"

I am sure Dr. Novelli knows this neighborhood restaurant, the Rodi in Vicente López and Ayacucho that is always packed with couples and large family parties. He will picture the setting of the story I am about to tell him.

"Carlos and I used to go there when we were in the mood for homemade food. Last night, when I was following the waiter to my table, I wished Carlos was with me, and when I sat down, I felt empty of him. My nostalgia morphed into anger when the server in black uniform refused to serve me a half an order of *asado,* our barbecue—despite the fact that all items on the menu are advertised as being abundant for two. I felt angry at him. But my anger soon passed. I got distracted by another anxiety of larger proportions, aching for Carlos. I needed to get up and walk, or engage in some form of movement or activity— sometimes action frees me from angst. The white paper napkin on the cotton tablecloth offered me an avenue; I began to write phrases as they were coming to my mind."

While talking with Dr. Novelli, I rummage through my big purse on the sofa next to me. I find the napkin and say, "I rewrote the phrases as free verse. Let me read them to you."

> *Perfume without aroma,*
> *White shadow,*
> *White dove riding on the wind,*
> *A stranger to myself,*
> *My self in grief*
> *Bits of my loved dead ones.*
> *My roots! Where are they?*

Right after I finish, Dr. Novelli remarks: "A perception of yourself having no place, no essence, no roots."

"No identity either. A perfume without aroma—"

"—is not a perfume," he completes my sentence.

I turn my internal gaze on, again, in the blank zone without external stimuli, where I receive free associations to the phrases I've just recited. A couple minutes later, words and images begin to form in my mind, and I begin to put them in perspective. White cloth: white shadow: white dove.

"White speaks to me," I say, pausing a few seconds. "It triggers memories of the first weeks after Carlos' death, when I saw, or dreamed, or sensed, a white light moving across the bedroom when I was falling asleep—in that transitional area between wakefulness and sound sleep. Carlos was visiting me as a white light—I believed he was. I would rise up in bed and call his name—'Carlos! Carlos!' No response. He was not there. It was disappointing. But I loved those few moments when my own sensations brought him to life.'"

"He wasn't there in reality," adds Dr. Novelli, "but he was somewhere."

"He was all over our ... *my* condo. It feels usurping calling 'mine' the home that used to be 'ours.' When he was alive, every inch of our home belonged to both of us."

Dr. Novelli asks: "How was Carlos 'all over' your condo?"

"Carlos was omnipresent in the condo because we chose its décor and furnishings together, we watched the same birds through its windows as they flew south for the winter. Nothing belonged to him or to me, everything was ours. Absolutely everything has his touch imprinted on it. Even over the phone there, like when my assistant Salu brings him up in conversation. Last night I phoned her to get a report about how things are at home in Portland. I asked if she had spoken to the white marble box that keeps Carlos' ashes. She still does. She told me about her last conversation with Carlos."

I get silent, unsure of whether to go on with Salu's prolific fantasy. I decide to tell him.

"Salu told her husband, 'I spoke with Don Carlos, but he didn't say anything; he was not here. He always goes where Beatriz goes. Now he is in Buenos Aires. He is taking care of her, like he always has.'"

I've noticed that Dr. Novelli, who was silent last session, is rather interactive today. I needed his silence last time; he provided a safe cocoon for me to express the ailments frozen in my upper chest at the base of my throat; it was important to let out the pent-up emotions, bring them to life—and to break the ice that held back in my inner tears. Today's session is happening on an entirely different level. Dr. Novelli is helping me dig deeper into emotions and conflicts that lie beyond my conscious perceptions.

With his words Dr. Novelli switches my gaze back to him: "You were telling me that something happens in Buenos Aires that does not happen in the United States." He pauses a bit, searching for a more direct question, and then says, "Let's talk about when you and Carlos met."

His question reminds me of the photo I put in my wallet before I left for Buenos Aires. I take it out in case Dr. Novelli shows interest in looking at it—I suspect he won't show interest because if he did, he would interrupt the flow of "my" session. And he doesn't. So I hold the photo and contemplate it. With pleasure.

"This photo was taken in Buenos Aires, before we were married. We are in our bathing suits, sunbathing on the beach. I was in my late teens and he was in his twenties, so in love, so full of dreams. It pleases me to no end that we made our dreams come true over the years. Well, I talked about this during one of our previous sessions. I don't want to repeat myself."

"Why did you choose this photo for your wallet before coming here?" Dr. Novelli asks, obviously trying to get me closer to the source of my anxiety when I eat alone in Buenos Aires—my preoccupation today, which he follows closely.

"It was small enough to fit inside." I treasure Carlos' handwriting on the reverse. It says, *I am sending this photo to introduce you to my future wife Beatriz.* It never got mailed. I have it now, instead of the person for whom it was intended.

My internal smile disappears when my musings transport me to those times. Thinking about them makes the image of Aida, Carlos' mother, appear in my mind—a somewhat anxious, attractive woman with a moon-shaped face and delicate features. I remember her wearing a straight gray flannel skirt and a rose cashmere sweater.

With a knot in my throat I bring her up, adding: "She wasn't supportive of our marriage."

I dab the tears under my eyes. I wonder if I shall talk about this. If it came into my mind, it must be significant.

Dr. Novelli's gentle voice engages me: "What is going on, Beatriz?"

"I am feeling sad. We did not have a celebratory wedding party, only a civil marriage ceremony and a luncheon for parents, grandparents, uncles, and aunts. You know, we were both agnostic: he was Jewish, and I was Catholic." The quavering of my voice is warning me I am about to step into sensitive territory—I must be prepared to cry. I realize that.

3. Elusive Encounters

Dr. Novelli encourages me to continue: "You said you were feeling sad."

"Carlos was troubled when his mother tried persuading him to marry within the faith when we were dating. I felt bad for the predicament he was in, and didn't want to make his life harder. But I trusted that he would figure out how to deal with Aida's conflict. I felt good about how Carlos handled the situation; he told her that I was the girl he wanted to marry and he was going to do it regardless."

I am stalling.

"You seem rather hesitant talking about Aida's rejection," says Dr. Novelli.

"Yes, I haven't revisited this place in a very long time, not since she died. Carlos considered that she needed time to get used to the idea. She was not coming from meanness. She had been raised in a conservative Jewish family, speaking Yiddish, acculturated in expectations that never got questioned. Her acceptance of a mixed-faith marriage, Carlos thought, was just a matter of time.

"After we got married, both parents became affectionate to me and treated me as the precious wife of their son. Carlos had been right: it was a matter of time."

I get silent thinking about Carlos' ability to resolve conflicts without a fight. Dr. Novelli's expression signals that he is working in concentrated silence too.

"It seems that you might have expected an encounter with Carlos in Buenos Aires," says Dr. Novelli, apparently zeroing in on what he thought was the central issue of today's session. "An encounter that did not happen."

What he says touches a sensitive spot, an internal turmoil. My mind races, my heart beats faster, tears run down my cheeks. I realize my body knows something that I don't know. I swallow to clear the lump in my throat, and wait until I am able to talk. But how can I talk about something I am not conscious of? Well, this is the reason I am here, in this therapy; like any other mortal I can't access the corners of my unconscious by myself. I remain *ensimismada*—with my gaze turned inwardly—until I reconnect with Dr. Novelli's eyes. For a few more seconds I marvel at the fact that he can put in words something I haven't thought about. This is a skill I've been trained to develop—which nonetheless feels magical when I am sitting in the patient's chair.

When I can talk, I ask Dr. Novelli: "Do you mean I've gone to restaurants with the unconscious expectation of finding Carlos? You have a point about looking for him because I did feel saddened by his absence when I walked into Rodi's last night. I recall peeking behind me for a fraction of a second, to see if Carlos was following me. And when I reached the table, I felt disappointed for another fraction of a second, when he wasn't there waiting for me. What I have been doing is sad. Yet it is what a lover would do, isn't it? I was looking for my sweetheart."

In silence I reflect that I am looking for him because I want him back, but also because I don't want him to be *sad* or *alone*. The source of those words came to my mind—*How sad, how alone remain our dead ones*—a verse from G.A. Becquer which I learned in high school. It had obviously made an imprint in my mind. I must have had a perception ever since of dead people being *sad* and *alone*.

"But," I ask Dr. Novelli, "why haven't I looked for him in movie theaters? We used to enjoy going to movies together. I couldn't wait for our post-movie discussions. We were a good team for dissecting films. He saw things I had missed and vice versa. But I recognize that dining in Buenos Aires was more special than any other activity we did together. We would do things apart during the day and would come together at dinnertime. It was so interesting to exchange our juicy stories of the city and all the surprises we had encountered when we least expected them. During the afternoon he may have seen documentaries at the art museum; I may have attended a psychoanalytic lecture. It makes sense that I would be looking for my other half in restaurants at dinnertime, here in Buenos Aires, where we met and married."

The encounter with Carlos that did not happen keeps feeling accurate; it is the source of my anxiety and feelings of deflation. Wanting to cry and smiling, I feel dumbfounded thinking that I've been looking for my Carlos unknowingly. I indulge in fantasizing that the young Beatriz finds the young Carlos as he is in the photograph, and they start a life together all over again. By the tightening I feel in my throat, I know it can't happen. I sink into silence. I feel despondent. Totally helpless.

Dr. Novelli breaks my silence: "What are you thinking about, Beatriz?"

"This photo takes me to a time when Carlos was healthy. Looking at him ... at *us* ... it brings me comfort."

I feel myself on the edge of discovery, as my attention drifts to pictures related to an accident, which he suffered at age fifty, when a truck hit him from behind as he was riding his bicycle. Carlos' chronic back pain had plagued him ever since, long before the acute cancer pain he suffered in the last years of his life. I am realizing that part of me is merged with Carlos in a state of pain. I want to share this revelation with Dr. Novelli.

"My heart is carrying a Carlos in a state of horrendous pain. He would not want me to do that." I get silent. Dr. Novelli is silent too.

"I am eager to look for photos of Carlos playing tennis, doing cross-country skiing, running, bicycling, swimming. Taking mud baths during his bicycle trips to California. Or that photo, which I have only in my mind, of him in his forties, getting up at 7 in the morning to run in Central Park during our Christmas vacation's freezing weather ... or that other photo, also in my mind, of him returning to the hotel room with a huge smile and a treat for me, a steaming hot chocolate I loved to sip in bed. I must remind myself that Carlos was more than pain, that he was a passionate person with a zest for life."

I feel closure now that I understand my anxiety over dining alone in Buenos Aires. Now my mind is going back to the beginning of the session, where something stray was left behind. What was it? As I get close to figuring it out, Dr. Novelli asks, "What is on your mind, Beatriz?"

"A thread is hanging loose," I say. "Earlier in the session, we talked about the ways I experienced being by myself at Rodi. What I said was grim. I was thinking about that."

Dr. Novelli says, "We were saying that when you are alone, in Buenos Aires, you feel blurred in life, having no roots, feeling like a shadow, like a perfume without aroma."

"It is grim!" I say again, angry at myself. "I would have never self-described in those terms when Carlos was alive."

"Beatriz," says Dr. Novelli, "you feel as if you really were blurred in life, as if you really *were* helpless facing life alone. This *is not* a reality. You *are not* blurred. You *are not* helpless. It is how you feel."

"I know this is not how I have been throughout my life," I say as if I hadn't heard him. Realizing I am being defensive I pause to consider what he just said. "I must admit, you have shown me ways in which I have presented myself in a diminished light. Why would I devalue myself after Carlos' death? Do I feel incomplete, as in the half-face selfies I've been taking? What comes to mind is the change from being 'two in seamless connection' to being 'one' without the other. It feels like having two parallel selves inside. Each self seems to have its own voice. One feels vulnerable, the other feels strong. One is my self in grief, and the other my enduring self. My grieving self sees me incomplete without Carlos and is insecure. I feel betrayed by my grieving self. I want my assertive old self to stand up and take over!"

I get lost in thought realizing the huge power of loss to change my self-image. I hope it is a temporary station in my grieving process.

Dr. Novelli moves forward in his chair.

Our time is up. I say goodbye with our usual handshake and exit—still in a pensive state.

The reflective space of the consulting room stays with me during the elevator ride. I see the photo in my wallet as what was once a real moment. I fly to that place and time, sunbathing and lingering next to Carlos. Who would have thought then, when we were dating, that my Carlos, that we, would one day be taken by surprise by the experience of death that caught us unprepared?

What now?

What now, Dr. Novelli?

When I step out of the elevator, the lobby is darker than usual. I can't see what is happening; the massive wood door blocks my view of Posadas Street. Once outside, I stand on the covered marble platform and go down five steps carefully—astonished at the early nighttime. Before reaching the sidewalk, I open the folded purple umbrella I carry in my purse at all times during the spring season in Buenos Aires. The sunny day has vanished, and now copious rain gets flung at my body sideways by the wind.

Mindlessly, I cross Callao Avenue and reach the opposite sidewalk soaking wet. By now my umbrella is dancing to the whims of the wind. Why not? I discard my cover and let the rain fall on me. Its coolness wakes my senses. By the time I get home the spring rain has stopped, and the afternoon sunlight announces its comeback. I feel more real.

4

Ripples of Loss

Where was Carlos to take my temperature?

No longer dizzy this morning, I sit up and get out of bed slowly. Last night I was sick for the first time since Carlos died. Where was he to figure out what's going on? To walk with me when I was unstable on my feet? To give me one of the pills he carried in his first aid bag? Feeling like a helpless child is embarrassing. How was I supposed get to a physician at night?

It dawns on me that in Buenos Aires I can go to any pharmacy. They function as first aid stations. I go to the nearest one, three blocks away, on Quintana and Callao. When I ask to be seen by the pharmacist, the receptionist answers: "The reason?"

"I want to have my blood pressure taken." After paying the one-dollar fee in advance, I sit and wait. He comes after thirty minutes and shows me to a tiny room with a medical examination table and a chair. I sit down on the chair while he stands with a tablet ready to write down my symptoms and history. As he starts asking questions, the child in me resents him for taking Carlos' place.

"What medications are you taking?"

I mention a couple.

"What are the dosages?"

I motion that I don't know.

"What is the brand?"

"I don't know, I don't know."

"How come you don't know the dosage?" My eyes get swollen with tears. "Could you call your doctor's office and ask?"

"I can't, my doctor is dead, and I don't know the doses or the brands because he was always with me, he knew all of that. My medications were prescribed in the United States so you would not know them if I told you their names. I am here temporarily."

Now the pharmacist is the one with the helpless expression.

"Would you take my blood pressure—I just want to know if something could be wrong with my heart."

"Are you taking any heart medication?"

"No, I am freaking out because my husband died seven months ago, this is my first time sick without him, and he was my doctor. Do you have a Kleenex, please?"

I take the tissue, look down and cry in silence. When I look up again his expression has softened, he says to place my arm on the bed and he takes my blood pressure. It's normal.

He recommends an over-the-counter herbal preparation—which Carlos would have opposed, since the composition of herbals is a mystery, while there is no mystery about medications approved by the FDA. I buy the herbal anyway because I am a placebo person; I can just look at it and feel cured.

When I get home to prepare for the day ahead, I put the bag down and take out the placebo. The package says it's for liver-related symptoms. I take it and feel immediately better. Carlos and I found it funny that many *porteños*—natives of Buenos Aires—suffer from their livers. We never heard people in the United States complain about their livers. We used to chuckle about this. As I take a shower and get dressed, this little episode makes me realize I must learn to give myself what I used to receive from Carlos—which was just about everything. I must learn to give myself more confidence, more protection, more encouragement. And flowers, I see as I look around preparing to leave: the apartment needs fresh flowers.

Dos Escudos has already seated the line of customers waiting for tables—only one tiny and isolated table is available next to the wall. There I am able to secure some small measure of privacy and quietude.

I feel comfortable in the culture of this café, even if it is small, even if open tables are hard to find at the hours when I typically arrive. It is unique in its fusion of quality food, attentive servers, laid-back attitude, and full rack of newspapers—all of it makes me feel pampered here. Comparing it to my other culture, I value how smoothly this place runs with unseen hands managing its daily operation.

I get up for a moment and return to my seat with *La Nación,* our oversized newspaper. I try to fold it to fit the space of the crowded little table already sporting marmalades, salt and pepper shakers, a framed stand with the daily menu, and an elegant paper placemat bordered by spotless silverware. While I skim the headlines about Argentina's political affairs, I only read deep in foreign news of interest—and the cartoon pages. Tute's cartoons are my dessert, he is my hero cartoonist with his *porteño*-psychoanalytic humor. I can't share them with my U.S. friends—what is funny to me as a native isn't funny to foreign visitors. Humor is a cultural byproduct.

Raising my eyes, I notice that thirty minutes have elapsed: the tables all remain filled, and more people are gathering at the door. I feel the guilt I learned in the States about occupying a table when other customers are waiting—it causes businesses to lose money. This isn't a cause for guilt in Buenos Aires.

I am just beginning my paper, working out a methodology to access the inner expressiveness of the tango. I give myself a pep talk to remain here and continue working: "Beatriz, why should you feel at fault when everybody lingers at cafés in this city? Don't you realize that Dos Escudos buys several copies of each newspaper because the management likes to offer unhurried time to its seated clients? They don't mind if people waiting for tables leave to go elsewhere." I appreciate this slow-paced culture—it doesn't feel greedy. I also appreciate that a glass of water isn't placed on my table immediately and that the bill is not delivered when I am still chewing my food. In the States we are trained to eat and run. Not here. Servers take their time before coming for orders; foreigners get impatient with our "inefficiency," not realizing that it's not a matter of efficiency—it's a less voracious cultural way of being. In the States we are also accustomed to clearing our tables in fast food restaurants—training which probably starts in school. That's why we adults behave like rats in a labyrinth, providing free cleaning to anonymous corporations that earn billions of dollars a year. Without the pennies we save them, they would have to hire actual cleaning personnel. Earlier this year, my grandchildren asked me to take them to Chipotle where they proceeded to clean the table after we ate. I asked them to stop and think about why they were cleaning the table for a restaurant. I presented my point of view and suggested we walk out without volunteering our free labor to Chipotle. Soon thereafter I read that the company's revenue for the year was $5.9 billion. Without guilt I can say that in Buenos Aires, the customers don't clean the tables.

I never felt "at fault" lingering for hours at this café during previous trips. Could this be one of the many ripples of my grieving state—"displaced guilt," as Dr. Novelli might say?

"Leisure is unique to the café culture of Buenos Aires"—this could be the title of an article I might type up sometime soon.

The male server, Martín, starts talking to me as he approaches my table.

"Good morning, Beatriz."

I order the usual macchiato and tell him I will have something else when I finish reading the paper. He brings the coffee. When I eventually put down the newspaper he comes back; I order a *frutos rojos* smoothie with orange juice—no water. We *porteños* like to adjust the food preparation to our desires—*Could you bring me the salad with olive oil? Could you bring me mashed potatoes instead of French fries? Could you double the amount of lemon juice for the fish—I prefer freshly squeezed lemon.* This can't be done in your average metropolis—not anymore.

Martín asks me how I would place my order in English. I say: "Red smoothie." He shows me "how bad" his pronunciation is: *Rrred esmuti.* We laugh. Martín has been spying on my typing, so he's figured out I speak English. I note he likes to befriend me. Although servers are very nice in the city, Martín slightly crosses a barrier—acting with more than the usual familiarity.

I get ready to pay and leave. I enjoy the casualness of not being addressed as madam or ma'am. He asks if I plan to come back this afternoon, like I sometimes do. I never know ahead of time, I say. Now he hurries up to the door to open it for me—servers don't open doors at cafés. I am out of training in being charmed, but I suspect that Martín wants to be noticed—more than as a server. I tell him, *Muy amable, gracias* (Thank you, kindly), and walk out to the street realizing that, so far, I've considered him "Martín the server." I tell myself something that wouldn't have crossed my mind when I was married: next time I will scan Martín as a single woman would. I feel naughty. I remind myself there is nothing to feel guilty about over a thought—guilt applies to actions and not to thoughts—and I am no longer married, so I can look at men "as men" if I want to without feeling at fault.

Once I step inside Dr. Novelli's office building, I am glad to see that one of the two small elevators—my waiting room of sorts—is waiting on the ground floor. I notice how these two extremely narrow elevators don't match the scale of this lobby; perhaps they were built after the initial construction, in the space that had been designed for a single spacious elevator which for some reason had to be demolished. I open its old, narrow type of folding metal door that gathers like a curtain. It seems adequate for one and a half persons, or for a single person overloaded and burdened by guilt. On the third floor, I ease open the noisy metal folding doors and close them as quietly as possible.

Ringing the bell of office 34 marks the beginning of my weekly internal adventure.

Dr. Novelli looks at me calmly from his chair as I lean forward a bit on the sofa.

"I want to know if I am working through my grief as I should. I've been wondering. How would I know? How far in the process am I?"

Dr. Novelli does not respond. I go on: "I've been asking myself this question since yesterday. Someone said to me, 'Being alone must have been difficult for you.' Although vague, my answer was exactly what I wanted to say. I mumbled that it had been difficult to transition from being 'Beatriz and Carlos' to being 'Beatriz,' but that coping with daily life by myself had been relatively uncomplicated."

"What concerns you about this, Beatriz?"

"My concern? That I don't show anything on the outside. If a stranger met me today, he wouldn't entertain the possibility that I lost the love of my life just nine months ago. No one can see inside me—unless I want them to. My mourning process has been internal. On the outside I've stayed pretty together—at least I believe I have. Have I?"

I pause. Grieving has been an odd process. I drink some water and go right back to my original question.

"Am I grieving as I am supposed to?"

4. *Ripples of Loss*

"How do you think grieving is supposed to be?" asks Dr. Novelli.

"Well … in graduate school I learned the Kübler-Ross model of the five stages of grief. They've never made sense to me. But grief was not my clinical specialty so I haven't concerned myself with the topic. I reviewed the Kübler-Ross stages last night and wrote them down: I have the note here in my bag. *Denial, anger, bargaining, depression, acceptance.* I didn't know what to do with that—but went through with the exercise. I experienced denial—but not just at the beginning. I experienced anger, but it wasn't related to grief—it was directed at the doctor who harmed Carlos while the harm was occurring. I've felt sadness—not depression. Acceptance began when Carlos and I assumed our fates jointly. And I don't recognize any bargaining stage or any moments of trying to negotiate with a higher power to avoid the inevitable."

Dr. Novelli asks a similar question again, trying to shift me from theory to my feelings: "What else are you questioning about your grieving?"

"I should have felt more desperate," I say. "I question why I don't cry outside the sessions—I expected I would cry every time I thought about Carlos. I anticipated that I would feel like a total emotional mess. I've had one regressive episode, last night at the pharmacy. I am also beginning to experience moments of happiness. What else am I questioning about my grief? I should have felt desperate, deeply depressed. I am confessing sins to you, Dr. Novelli. The sins of not feeling as terrible as expected after losing the love of my life."

I feel like a fly that buzzes around a room but neither lands nor leaves.

The word "sin" takes me to age eleven, my hair made into two braids by my mother's perfectionist hands, feeling terrified as I knelt on the step of the confessional at the Iglesia del Sagrado Corazón in my old neighborhood of Barracas. At church I was assumed to be a guilty sinner.

"Dr. Novelli, how come I feel mostly okay?"

After thinking a moment, Dr. Novelli responds: "There are many ways to grieve, Beatriz. Besides, Carlos advised you to be happy, to make sure you did *only* what you liked to do, so you would not stay sad after he was gone."

I relish the soothing effect that Carlos' words have on me—even if Dr. Novelli is the one saying them.

"Without his words, I would have felt guilty about smiling, about laughing, about eating, about dancing, about having a good time. I can easily access Carlos' words through memory, or place my hands at the base of my throat—the part of my body where I've decided he lives. In my 'Carlos and Beatriz' place, he and I stand solidly together. He is still protecting me. He doesn't want me to feel guilty. He said it unequivocally, he wants me to be happy."

"You have a good memory of Carlos. He is with you," Dr. Novelli comments. "You are going through a grief process with certain characteristics: feeling okay, not feeling overwhelmed by pain or sadness. You could consider yourself fortunate to be grieving in this manner."

Dr. Novelli has normalized what I believed wasn't normal. How many are still reading the Kübler-Ross model and feeling that their grief is not the process it should be? I am glad to learn that my grief is my own improvised dance, that I am not supposed to follow a choreography.

I regroup, internally sensing that another question is forming. As it becomes clear to me, I ask it.

"Dr. Novelli, does the fact that I cried so much during the 'eulogy session,' after such a long period of dryness, mean that something hardened inside me, to the extent that *only* the heart-wrenching eulogy could make my tears flow again?"

Dr. Novelli gives me a nonverbal "no" with his head.

"Maybe I don't feel as much as I did before," I insist. "Could my heart have frozen after watching Carlos suffer so much?"

I stop, dreading that Dr. Novelli will tell me I have lost my feelings. I breathe; I drink water; I brace myself inside, and in the silence I continue.

"His suffering was too much for him to bear and too much for me to witness." I repeat what I just said slowly—as if I need to own how tragic that was. "Too much for him to bear and too much for me to witness."

Now that I am done talking, he speaks.

"I don't think you lost your feelings. There is not just one way to grieve, Beatriz. Your way has been alternating between crying seasons

54

and drought seasons. You are a little tearful today, and you may be interpreting your periods of not crying as forgetting Carlos and feeling guilty about that."

What he says makes me pause. The fear of forgetting Carlos has hounded me since he died. When I don't cry, I feel afraid that I will eventually forget him.

"When Carlos died, I had a type of crying spell unknown to me before. At his death his body was rigid, but it did not prevent me from laying my head on his chest, sobbing and talking to him. I was disconsolate. I laid on his chest, howling from a place I didn't know was in me. During the five following months I cried convulsively, especially at night when I went to bed alone, having no Carlos to console me. I could not console myself by thinking he was in a better place, watching over me. I had tears then. No question about that."

I raise my eyes to engage Dr. Novelli's. I feel held, contained by his blue eyes. I continue.

"The morning after he died, I cried with a friend who had followed my emotional 'mini-downs' and 'maxi-downs' throughout Carlos' illness. She is a psychoanalyst and the best equipped person to understand how desperate and disconsolate I was. Rachel is her name. She lives all the way across the country, yet she held me close during Carlos' worst times. As a physician, she could assess Carlos' medical condition. Rachel called the morning after his death when I had frantically finished throwing away all the pain medications I could find at home. I was alone, bursting at the seams, growling and hitting the bathroom counter with my fist—when Rachel's voice on the phone stopped my acting out. I said hello and crawled on her lap. Carlos' handkerchiefs, scrunched up in my hands, didn't last me but a few minutes. I had to put Rachel on hold to go get a bath towel so I could dry the fluids coming out of my mouth, nose, and eyes. I sounded like a child talking, weeping, and drying her face and nose—all at the same time. I am sure Rachel could not make out what I was saying. And I don't remember. I do remember my gratitude for her calling me at the precise time I needed arms around me. The arms I will no longer get from Carlos."

I pause to attend to the flashbacks now coming to mind with such a sense of urgency it's like they are asking to be told to Dr. Novelli.

"I wasn't at my mother's side when my father died; we were on two different continents. It happened when Verita and I had just returned to the States after being with them for a month in Buenos Aires. I wanted to visit while he was not very sick, so he could see Verita; I knew how much it would mean to him. After he saw her and gave her a loving smile, he whispered to me: 'Thank you for bringing her, I can die now.' During that month, Bernardo was getting neither better nor worse; his physician said he was stable and could live for six more months in that condition. Verita was in fourth grade, and we left for the States so she could go back to school, and as soon as we boarded the flight home, Bernardo took a turn for the worse. He had to be rushed to the hospital. He waited until I left to protect me from his death—I know that in my heart. When we got home about forty hours later, I called my mother: the person who answered the phone told me my father had died.

"Elena did not want to speak to me that day, or any day I called her after that. I had failed her by not turning around and going back to Buenos Aires to support her. I failed to grasp the depth of her tragedy by not making her my priority. She and I confronted this moment years later, when she accepted our offer to come visit us. She covered her profound hurt with hot anger. I feel glad that she said all she had to say. I had no excuses to offer but I apologized to her for not having returned to Buenos Aires to be by her side."

Now in silence, with tears flowing down my cheeks, I see my father's happiness when he saw Verita, I see my deeply wounded mother years later, I see Carlos containing her in his embrace. And I see me, carrying the heaviest of guilts, and learning the life lesson of never again failing to make decisions with my heart. When family or friends are vulnerable, and need you by their side, everything else can wait. After a long pause, I signal to Dr. Novelli that I am ready to go on.

"Going back to Rachel, and being together with her that day, took my relationship with her to another level. I think it bonded us for years to come. I had tears then too. No question about that. Later they dried up. I need to change the subject now."

Dr. Novelli: "Today you have been worrying about not crying for several months."

"Yes," I said. "I cried easily during the first five or six months, mostly in solitude. A few times in company. But for three months before I arrived in Buenos Aires, I could only cry when someone asked me about Carlos and I had to say: 'He died.' Just before I left Portland, Malina, who is a server at McCormick's, a café across the street from *our* home ... from *my* home ... she spotted me across the tables and walked toward me waving and smiling. We kissed and she immediately asked about Carlos: 'I have not seen him for at least a year,' she said. I took a deep breath and began to talk; my voice came out as a raspy murmur. 'Carlos died nine months ago,' I whispered. Malina covered her mouth with both hands, her face got a bit disfigured, and she cried out: 'I loved him.' We embraced and wept together until someone called her from one of the tables. We took our time to separate. We looked at each other and I whispered some more to her, 'I want you to know that Carlos was especially fond of you, and of your twin little girls.' Now customers from two tables were calling Malina. She had to go, but before leaving she wrote her phone number on a piece of paper and encouraged me to call her. She offered to come to my place. 'We could look at Carlos' photos, or just talk.' For nearly four months, June through September, I no longer cried. So, yes, Dr. Novelli, I've been worried I had lost all my tears."

"Do you remember crying since you arrived in Buenos Aires?" asks Dr. Novelli.

"No, not really. Just recently I was having a drink with Yael, a friend from the States who was vacationing in Buenos Aires. We talked about inconsequential matters and suddenly we paused. We looked at each other in silence. She said: 'It has to be so hard for you to lose the love of your life.' She leaned forward, caressed my arm, held my hand, her face turned red, water filled her eyes. It felt odd that she was crying and I wasn't. She told me how lucky I had been, having had a long marriage with the love of my life. Many women, she said, don't know what that is. She is not the first woman to tell me this."

Dr. Novelli: "You have been measuring your connection to him by the presence or absence of your crying. And you are feeling a little guilty about that."

"I agree, I do have a little guilt about being afraid to forget Carlos," I tell Dr. Novelli, "little compared to the 'big guilt' I felt about my mother."

"Don't Be Sad When I'm Gone"

Dr. Novelli: "The guilt about your mother may be more complicated; you had an ambivalent relationship with her, and this deserves more attention. Today you are crying about your father's death, and about not being by your mother's side. You are reassuring yourself that you still have your tears."

I retreat for a moment.

"You are right about my little guilt. I began feeling unusually guilty at Dos Escudos today, for staying too long at my table. And for entertaining 'naughty' thoughts about men. In the elevator I had the fantasy of being overweight with guilt, and during this session I imagined being a guilty sinner at age eleven. I've felt guilty all over the place, and you are narrowing it down to the important underlying guilt I feel for not crying more about Carlos."

I can tell that our time is up. As I rise from the moss green couch and walk to my right, where Dr. Novelli stands opening the door for me, I tell myself what I didn't say in the session. Dr. Novelli's therapy has made my grief easier to bear.

We shake hands until next week, and I am sad to leave.

Twelve feet down the narrow hallway, I call my miniature elevator.

Cozy enough for one and a half persons.

Today, it is just adequate for me and the ripples of guilt that undulate in circles around me.

5

Where Did My Self-Esteem Go?

The outdoors calls me on this perfect, balmy afternoon with its deep blue skies, but a loud noise inside the apartment startles me—something I haven't heard before. Soon I realize the unusual racket is coming from outside the living room window. I race over to the glass but stop in my tracks halfway there, and tiptoe closer, until I see what all this "something" is about: two feisty doves are zealously poking each other with their beaks. They pause and puff their chests out like boxers in a ring about to resume the fight. Are the birds really fighting? It is spring—I could be watching courtship and procreation. A strictly urban person, I silently sneak over to my laptop to look up "doves + mating + behavior + season." Indeed, male and female doves, at this time of year, romance each other like the ones I am watching now. Twenty minutes later the doves on my windowsill are kissing incessantly, now flapping their wings, now flying from my perch to another, now coming back to my sill for more urgent kissing.

Birth in the animal realm and green renovation are the mandates of the spring. In a certain sense, I am fulfilling my own mandate of renewal, opening up to a life that I now see from a single woman's vantage point. By necessity, my renewal will engender new ways of thinking—new ways of being in the world. What will those new ways be?

I am feeling hungry for breakfast, and for greenery and open space—three things not easily found together in this metropolis. But I know where I can find them, five blocks from here. I head to the historical café La Biela, an outdoor venue founded in the 1880s that overlooks two parks punctuated by the ancient colossal *ombú* trees.

"Don't Be Sad When I'm Gone"

As I walk through the streets, I think over my story with Gustavo from its beginning in this city, when I was a graduate student. Vague snapshots of our friendship come to mind, and of our brief dating that came to an abrupt end when I met Carlos. Our lives didn't cross for decades after I left Argentina. We reconnected ten years ago, when Carlos and I bumped into him at pizzeria Guerrin in Avenida Corrientes. This was when Carlos and I began traveling to Buenos Aires once a year so that I could do much-needed research for my book about tango. Gustavo and I kept in loose touch since the Guerrin encounter. During my later trips, we would meet up for a *cafecito*—which implies "conversation" in Buenos Aires—so we've stayed updated with our major life events, and our annual exchange of birthday greetings helped us maintain our loose contact.

Our companionship now has taken some turns for the worse. But now that I stride up to the outdoor café tables under their great parasols, both my walk and my musings will have to wait.

To sit at an outdoor table here in the upscale Recoleta neighborhood is akin to being at a theater and not knowing what show will take the stage. I know that someone with heartwarming art will enact the performance: that couple of street tango dancers, maybe; or the male *bandoneón* player; the male violinist; the female singer from the Andes mountains. I turn my head and watch the humans of Buenos Aires as they parade by on the La Biela sidewalk, with family elders, baby carriages, children, dogs. Locals lean back in their chairs with their faces turned up like flowers to maximize their exposure to the sun—getting an early spring tan is a priority. In weather like this, the sun's carcinogenic effects may just be a consideration one postpones for cloudy winter days. People strolling unhurriedly along the sidewalk or beside the park, or just sitting back at their leisure, get juxtaposed in my mind with Seurat's *La Grande Jatte*—adjusted for time and urban setting.

One of La Biela's servers sees me from afar, and he approaches me with a smile and an expression of surprise. I was hoping he'd be on duty today. We kiss on the cheek, and he immediately asks: "Where is the *muchacho?*" I cannot verbalize the words *he died*; with my hand covering my mouth I move my head from side to side conveying *I can't talk*. Tears fill my eyes. I can tell he understands. He sheds tears too and embraces me in silence. "Carlos appreciated you so much," is all I am able to whisper. "I loved him too," Miguel says as he dries his tears with his handkerchief. We remain silent for a minute in Carlos' honor. "Is there anything I can do for you, Beatriz?" he asks with an air of normalcy. I order a tenderloin sandwich in pita bread, with lettuce and tomatoes, no fries, and say: "Thank you, Miguel. I've known you for ten years, you are the best in your profession."

The outdoors is so spectacular that I want to be looking up this afternoon. My laptop, which normally travels inside my big purse, may not get to see the light today. Miguel brings the food and periodically comes back just to chat and keep me company. I ask him about his children; his gesture of being overwhelmed says everything. He does say that the hardship of sending them to private schools is killing him. I empathize with Miguel wanting the best education for his children and stretching his waiter's salary to get it done. I can tell he feels sad and protective of me.

The singer is tuning her guitar. I look up and see her arranging her paraphernalia on the ground, under the giant *ombú* tree whose canopy shades the entire La Biela courtyard. Its massive branches have to be cut often, since they reach forty or fifty feet in length and would interrupt the heavy traffic on narrow Quintana Avenue. Back to the singer who is beginning her show. She plays an old sweet bolero which Carlos and I danced in Buenos Aires when I was seventeen, at a little club where he took me on our first date, on a Saturday afternoon—in the late 1960s, people under eighteen were not admitted to bars or clubs at night, so Buenos Aires' upscale suburbs Vicente López and Olivos had several afternoon venues. In the next piece, *"Qué será, será"* (Whatever will be, will be), the singer's voice and her sweet Andean look are captivating. I rise and walk over to where she is playing, and stand just a few feet in front of her as she sings these lyrics depicting the journey through life from childhood, to falling in love, to becoming parents. The expression is used when one accepts that fate will decide the outcome of an unchangeable situation.

We exchange glances and smiles. The rest of her potential audience is lounging in La Biela's courtyard from which only a few people can see her. When the song ends, I lean over to place a generous tip in the man-type hat that Andean women wear. With a big smile on her face, she hands me a CD with her recorded songs. This is her thank you. She asks me to stay for her next song. I do, and my heart dissolves listening to her voice sing *"Bésame mucho"*—as it blends into Nat King Cole's rendition, back at that club, Atelier, when I was only 17, drinking Coca-Cola, and being impressed with the elegant venue Carlos had chosen for our date.

When the song ends, I tell her: "Your song and your voice carried me to poignant remembrances, the times I was falling in love with the man of my life." I return to my table in the courtyard and stay another hour sitting in the same chair, connecting in tenderness with Carlos and our first kisses at Atelier, the venue with reddish-orange interior lighting. I am also connecting with him from this chair at La Biela where we spent thousands of hours "just being together." This year I am "just being"—and hurting from his absence. I well up a little and take a deep breath. If he were here, we could together conjure up Nat King Cole in duet with this Andean woman, and rejoice at the evocation of the old Atelier. I would have wanted to know his memories of that date.... I don't remember talking about Atelier with him. I remember wearing a light yellow-creamy A-line coat, in an Audrey Hepburn style for the fall, which my mother Elena—the family tailor—had made for me. Elena's handiwork takes me into another nostalgic journey. *"Las manos de mi madre"* (My mother's hands) was the title of her eulogy....

My phone alarm says that my session starts in twenty minutes.

This afternoon I am an overlapping of past and present—well, we all are. The past molds us. But pasts have different weights in our present identities. The past we shared with a beloved partner through an entire lifetime has more weight than a past visit to the Great Wall of China. My future identity will probably be weighted heavily by who I became in my relationship with Carlos, and only lightly weighted by my sole experiences in the many occurrences that I will soon know—and which he will never know.

Unlike I usually do, today I enter Dr. Novelli's office lobby already *ensimismada*—absorbed in my thoughts. I've been cogitating for several hours. Already on the third floor, I encounter Dr. Novelli as he meets me at the door with his blue eyes—my calming containers, my line of connection with him, my grief and my spring renewal.

~~~

5. *Where Did My Self-Esteem Go?*

I step into my sanctuary of self-examination, where from session to session we have been unmasking the inner adversaries that obstruct my path to a healthy life.

"Dr. Novelli, I can't believe that my inability to write for two solid years changed overnight after discussing the problem with you. I gave no further thought to our discussion. I can't even remember what we said, but whatever we explored changed something in me that night during my sleep. The unexpected happened the following morning, when I was going from the bedroom to the bathroom, thinking about brushing my teeth. In that narrow hallway I saw a sign in my mind, with the title and content of the book I wanted to write. This was astounding to me since I had not come here with the intention to write a book." With a smile I add, "You must be a very good therapist." He thanks me and smiles too.

I reflect. Sometimes therapy leads to rapid changes, like the spring's explosion of greenery. The unexpected reawakening of my creativity and the melting of my tears are two cases of that sudden effect.

"Ah—I also chose the title and created the outline for that paper I told you about: 'Tango, an Internal Dance.' I added to the methodology section the idea that most popular dances are 'extroverted,' and observers may watch the feelings portrayed in their expressions—whereas in tango, dancers are introverted, showing no feelings others can see; their expressivity is internal. I also went through some photographs showing how inexpressive the faces of tango dancers can be, compared to the highly expressive faces of modern dancers who seek to portray ideas and emotions through their powerful gestures and movements. I know I'll be ready to present it on November 13."

With obvious gladness, Dr. Novelli remarks: "Creativity helps the grieving process, Beatriz."

"The *problem* is," I say, "that ever since the morning I really began writing again, I've been unable to stop. It has been all I've wanted to do. Exclusively. I went from the extreme of no writing at all for two years to the extreme of writing until I dropped. It is *ridiculous*. I also feel torn apart between staying home to write or going out with friends when invitations come. Isn't this *pathological?*"

Dr. Novelli: "How did you feel *torn apart?*"

"Don't Be Sad When I'm Gone"

"Here is how I felt torn apart. My musician friends and I had made plans to go to San Telmo for lunch before one of them, Beau, was to return to the States. We had dinner the night before; I was excited about getting together again. I took a cab to the restaurant in San Telmo, but a torrential storm got the cab stuck in a jam shortly after I left home. Avenida 9 de Julio looked like an immense parking lot; traffic wasn't moving as far as I could see. I phoned Beau who was with the others at the restaurant, and we agreed I would not make it on time before he had to depart for the airport. I told the taxi driver to take me back home, feeling delighted I was returning to my writing. I was also delighted about meeting my friends again. This is how I felt torn—equally pulled by something social and by writing."

Dr. Novelli: "Beatriz, when you think that your writing is a 'problem,' or that it is 'ridiculous' that you can't stop writing, or that you are in conflict—as feeling 'torn apart' implies—you are devaluing the re-encounter with your writing: you are devaluing your creativity. The book you are working on gives you many emotional moments. It brings you an internal pleasure. Doesn't it?"

"Gustavo would agree with you. He tells me I can't postpone a passion; I must do it when it calls me."

"The writing and the social calls don't have to exclude one another," Dr. Novelli adds. "Could you enjoy your friends without feeling bad because you are not writing? Could you enjoy your writing without feeling bad because you are not with your friends? This is the idea."

I feel immensely relieved that Dr. Novelli is demolishing the stress I created around writing. The pleasure it gives me is too important. I don't want to lose it.

Dr. Novelli continues: "By the way, you are doing much better than when you started therapy. How do you feel about these changes, Beatriz?"

"I haven't noticed my own changes," I admit. "Well, I am more internally at peace for longer periods of time, sometimes the entire day. I made a new friend, Joel. He is a classical and ballroom dancer. We have a cordial relationship. He introduced me to his friends. I enjoy them all."

I enter musing mode again. It's hard to face that I've devalued my "good things" by calling them *ridiculous, pathological,* and so on. Well … that's why I choose to do therapy: I cannot see myself clearly. We all have blind spots—until a therapist points them out to us. But I don't see my self-devaluing in front of others. I believe I still present myself as a worthy person, as I always had—before Carlos died. This self-perception that doesn't match the way I have been all my life—it may be one of those ripples of grief that will take time to change. This morning, at the park, I dwelled on the past and present as overlapping internal experiences as well as separate moments in time. I can't wait for this alien self-disparagement to clear up as my therapy progresses.

"It would be helpful if you could say what you are thinking," says Dr. Novelli.

"Yes, Dr. Novelli. I was going back to those instances when you pointed out my lowered self-esteem. One instance was when I was talking with you about my professional life: I told you which degrees I have in psychology, and my work as a clinical psychologist in private practice. Then at a later time, I referred to my teaching, and you asked me to elaborate. I did, and told you that teaching had always been part of my practice as well as publishing in peer-reviewed journals. You asked me for details and I said that my last teaching was at a psychoanalytic institute based in New York with a branch in Kansas City. It was then that you pointed out how I had left significant achievements out of my initial presentation.

"Another instance was when the verses I wrote at Rodi's revealed a self-perception I wasn't aware of. I saw myself as 'perfume without aroma.' I can't believe I have been so unaware. I told my niece Roxana that I was working on my perceived self-devaluation in therapy. She laughed. 'Bea,' she said, 'you've always presented yourself as self-confident. Is your shrink smoking something?' She and I laughed. This self-devaluation is so subtle that *only you* can see it clearly, Dr. Novelli. I can see it clearly if I open my psychologist's eyes. I am the author of what I say."

I pause to go inside myself again, and proceed to share where my thoughts are taking me.

"Dr. Novelli, my self-devaluation seems to be one of the many odd experiences of this mourning process. I've never been a person with low self-esteem, or shy, or retreating. We talked about this when I was taking selfies of half my face. At a dance the other night, I was sitting next to my friend Virginia from San Francisco, whispering in her ear: 'See that dancer at the far end of the salon? The one wearing a silk blue shirt. He is an excellent *tanguero* who used to like dancing with me years ago at Club Español. He doesn't even look at me now.' As I was saying this, I saw him coming in our direction. I told Virginia: 'He is going to invite you, not me, for sure.' And there was his blue silk shirt standing in front of me, inviting me to dance. He said he came to my table because I wasn't responding to his long-distance invite."

"Beatriz, how do you see yourself?" asks Dr. Novelli.

"I like how my writing is shaping up. I wrote three stories. I feel satisfied. Writing enhances my self-esteem now." Dr. Novelli waits in silence. I do the same.

Dr. Novelli: "You are describing what you generate, not how you see yourself." He waits again for me to say something, but my mind is blank, so he adds: "I think you know more than what you said."

"When men or women tell me I am attractive, I don't believe it."

"Did you believe Carlos when he said you were attractive?"

"Yes, I believed everything he said," I respond.

It has been a long session. Time is up.

Dr. Novelli and I say goodbye until our next session, an entire week from now. As we shake hands at the door, I add: "Although our time is up, I want to mention that I feel inspired writing in Buenos Aires, so yesterday I changed my December return ticket for one in mid–February. The two-month extension will be better for therapy, too, I think."

With a nod and a smile, Dr. Novelli shows me that he concurs with my decision.

In my elevator-transitional zone, I reflect as I did when I was coming in. I repeat what I put together. I was seeing Carlos as the strong one in the unity we were, and since he vanished, I've unconsciously felt incomplete. I've seen myself as insufficient. I've invented rejections that did not exist. If Carlos could talk, he would tell me I will soon feel congruently capable, as I always felt when we were together. He would also tell me I gave him as much strength as he gave me.

5. *Where Did My Self-Esteem Go?*

As the doors of the elevator open, I walk out with my session at my back, cross the lobby, and step out to the streets where people stroll unhurriedly along the sidewalks and beside the parks. Instantly I become one more person strolling among the rest, embraced by this mother metropolis. I am one among three million others in the present, one among many more millions since the 1500s who have kept alive the look in the eye, the kind word to a stranger, the moment of pure being with each other.

6

I Carry a Horror
in My Heart

Spring in Buenos Aires.

Snowing in my heart.

Memories of the day Carlos died tormented me last night. I was trying to hold on to the details and emotions we felt on that 21st of December last year, from the time we got up in the morning until his body was wheeled away from our home.

I can't wait to get to my session today. It is three hours from now. I am walking to Dos Escudos, the corner café. The idea of being around other people suits me well at this moment; I welcome any distraction from the stabbing of my memories.

I sit at the solitary open table. There are three women servers: one of them smiles warmly when she sees me and comes my way. Carlos used to jest with her. As she approaches, I look at her, enjoying her kindness. I wish Carlos was with me to enjoy her too. Her name is Lucy; she would undoubtedly chat with me today, but I don't feel chatty. I order a smoothie and the usual macchiato and a croissant for later, when I am done with coffee.

It is brunch time for me. I open *La Nación* while I wait for my drink, but I can't concentrate on the newspaper. Martín, the male server, makes a point of leaning over as he passes by my table and mumbles something to me. He is playful, but today I don't feel playful so I don't ask him to repeat what he said. In a later "outing" to my table (he is not serving my section), he asks: "Are you ready to order?" I place the rest of my order with him: "Two *bocaditos* with cream-cheese and salmon." I am deeply immersed in my own world—*ensimismada,* as we say. Wrapped up in my thoughts.

I eat and pay the nearest server. I feel ready to move on. The red and green walls inside Dos Escudos feel distant; I half-close my eyes and make them blur. When I exit, the outside world feels quite far away too—in the distance.

Self-absorbed in hurting memories, I depart on automatic pilot and come back to crisper reality five blocks later, in the small elevator that takes me to the third floor. Facing Dr. Novelli's office, I stare at the bell. My lifeless index finger rings, the door opens, I motion hello to Dr. Novelli, and step inside my sanctuary. Seated in my safe corner of the sofa, I feel more fortunate than ever to be here. I have not said out loud to anyone what I am about to tell him today.

"I feel very fortunate to have you in my life," I say to Dr. Novelli with some trepidation.

"I am glad, Beatriz," he replies warmly.

"I have been postponing talking with you about the day Carlos died. Can't stall any longer. Can't bear this alone any longer. I had torturous flashbacks last night. I relived the worst day of my life. My skin feels too thin."

I pause, apprehensive about venturing any further.

Dr. Novelli encourages me to go on. "Don't be afraid, Beatriz," he says. "We'll tackle this together."

"I cried myself to sleep last night. I am giving myself no choice but to thrust ahead and name the last stop of Carlos' *vía crucis,* here, right now, with you."

I take a few deep breaths; I hold on to the bottled water in my lap, rather than setting it on the floor—my extra security blanket. Then I proceed.

"The medical system to which Carlos dedicated his professional career failed him. But this is for another session. I am still stalling." I look up at Dr. Novelli.

"All feelings are good," says Dr. Novelli with conviction. "Welcome them. The more you feel, the better."

So I start again, feeling reassured that Dr. Novelli won't let me drown.

"Metastasis had taken over his entire body.

"Once his recovery chances were zero and his days counted, Carlos took charge of his destiny. He faced his death with strength and without fears. He opted not to linger through a drawn-out, natural death. I know he did not want to impose the burden of a prolonged agony on us. I also know he had suffered enough. Having been at his side around the clock, as wife and nurse, I knew how bad his pain was. It gives me chills to remember how he described his pain to doctors: 'Knife stabbings into my back, no let-up, not even for a moment, sometimes lasting for hours.'

"This pain didn't attack like other kinds of pain he had before. This one was mean. Vicious. Cruel.

"He had signed up for medically assisted death under the Oregon law called *Death with Dignity*. It permits a physician to write a lethal prescription for terminally ill, mentally competent adults who have six months to live or less. Carlos had to prove he was mentally competent, and make two verbal requests, plus one in writing, to show that he had made the decision over a period of time. The verbal requests had to be made fifteen days apart, to confirm that the decision was not made on a whim. The day of the procedure he had to be able to drink from a cup by himself, and pass a mental status examination. The law required it.

"We had filled out the required application to the state. Carlos did not want to consider home hospice; as a physician he was familiar with it. After Carlos died, I used to look back at the options we had when he was told he had four weeks to live. My stressed mind tried to answer questions that had no answers. Would hospice have been a less traumatic option? I was wavering about decisions we had made together. I had to remind myself that Carlos participated actively in his treatment. This became my mantra for some time after his death:

We signed up for Death with Dignity *after long joint discussions. Carlos was an active participant in his own treatment, always.*

"Writing about these memories now has reminded me of a trauma Carlos suffered in 1965—two years after we first arrived in the States. His father called from Buenos Aires announcing that Aida, Carlos' mother, had been diagnosed with breast cancer, already metastasized in her liver. She was expected to die within a short period of time. Carlos and I were going through the happiest of times, enjoying my sixth month of pregnancy, and celebrating the prospect of having our baby girl in our arms in three short months. Although his internship at the Chicago Medical School would have to be interrupted for an unknown period of time, the choice was clear to Carlos. He was always clear about his heart's choices and made them with conviction. He wanted to be by his mother's side as her son, and he thought he could help her medically around the clock as well. We agreed it would be best for us to go together. So we packed and left for Buenos Aires at once.

"We rented an apartment next to his parents' home. One night I woke up at the sound of his footsteps: I anticipated his walking into our bedroom, and sat up to greet him, but he looked at me with marks of pain all over his face. He was sobbing and holding his head with one hand. I jumped out of bed and hugged him tightly, as he was crying. 'Mamá died,' he said.

"By this time, it was late in December. I had been wrapped up with our baby girl, Vera, who had been born exactly one month before Aida's death.

"Birth and death became strangely associated in our small apartment ... probably due to this association, Carlos grew excessively concerned with protecting Vera from germs. He allowed only family in the apartment—for short visits. When people beyond family came to visit, he had disposable face masks with elastic ear loops for them to wear inside the apartment.

"In my confinement with Vera during the prior month, I had not noticed the trauma Carlos was living daily, watching his mother become skin and bones over a three-month period of time. Aida died in his arms, while he was giving her a morphine injection to ameliorate her last hours. Her dying in his arms broke Carlos' heart. His resolve thereafter, as well as mine, was never to put our family though the same torment. We agreed on this explicitly some years later.

"It was fortunate for us that we had moved to the state of Oregon, where physician-assisted death had been legal for decades."

"Don't Be Sad When I'm Gone"

At this point in the session I was feeling the need to regroup before tackling the hardest memories a person can carry. Only Vera and I knew the details of the day he died. We are the only witnesses of how the physician-assisted death happened. I ask Dr. Novelli where the bathroom is, since I had never seen one in the office. I need to get up and move around more than I need to go to the bathroom.

"It's right behind you, to the left around the wall."

When I return to the sofa, Dr. Novelli asks with a note of concern in his voice: "How are you feeling, Beatriz?"

"Weak. But I can go on now.

"Back to the day he died. Carlos got up that morning and told me he could not wait another day for his pain to end. He still carried himself with strength of spirit, and with his characteristic dignity. Days before, he had told me he had only one reason for not wanting to die: I was that reason—he wanted to continue loving, caring for, and protecting me. But he needed to die, he explained. I knew he needed to die, I told him. We had fought it fiercely as long as we could. Now we were both resigned to fate with acceptance.

"That morning, Carlos was weaker than the day before, and so thin that his bones showed under his skin. I helped him move around, wishing the day nurse would arrive soon, afraid I wouldn't be able to hold him if he fell. Once he arrived, together we helped Carlos take the shower he insisted on having. We got him dressed as he laid on the bed. He chose what he wanted to wear and said he wanted to be helped to my recliner in the master bedroom, which he had seldom used.

"He was exhausted after the shower but alert; he exchanged some words with Vera and then some with me. As the hours passed, he either closed his eyes or looked longer and longer out the window, to the unending sky and the clouds, to the river and bridges, and to the mountains. He was detaching. Once in a while he complained about the doctor's lateness; I explained that the doctor was going to arrive at noon, as he had said. Carlos had waited for three hours in my recliner before the doctor arrived. He remained there throughout the early morning; and during the noon procedure, when he stopped breathing; and until the funeral home people came for him.

"I liked that he chose my chair; I will always wonder why he did. He must have felt closer to me in the chair infused by the scent of my body and my energy. It was smaller than his own, so it contained him better.

"Vera and I did what we needed to do. She kept her sanity; I managed to keep my strength, at least until the moment he died. We wanted to be our best, she for her dad, I for the love of my life. We accomplished that. He was serious without drama. Vera and I followed his lead. We were seriously solemn that morning—we didn't cry about him. Watching his unwavering commitment to leaving life behind on his own terms, and seeing no signs of regret on his part, helped me reach a new level of peace with *our* decision to end his life.

"Let me back up to the early morning of that day. A feeling of insanity dominated our home, as the madness of the pharmaceutical industry and the medical establishment descended upon our lives. It doesn't seem so monstrous in the territory of the professional medical world; it's part of the package society has gotten us to normalize. But when the pharmaceutical and medical worlds invade our private homes, even for doctors they exude a putrid smell.

"Carlos' final medication had to be purchased early in the morning on the same day. It was required by law. Vera drove to the indicated laboratory with a prescription for 100 capsules of Seconal, a sleeping medication more than 80 years old. When taken in a high dose, it brings about a coma in five minutes and death within 25 minutes. She carried a check for $3,500—the price of this prescription in 2017. Eight years before, it cost less than $200, but the laws had changed to allow for prices to be doubled and doubled again.

"We began the day inhaling the fetid greediness of the pharmaceutical industry. In this case it was the excessive price of an old drug, which costs practically nothing to produce after being on the market for so many years. It is morally wrong to profit so shamelessly from death, Vera and I commented, while Carlos continued to detach. In normal times he would have joined our rant, but his mind was turning elsewhere. For the first time in our lives as a family, his feelings were inaccessible to us. His presence-in-absence reminded me how transparent we had always been with one another. I didn't ask him what was on his mind because he needed peace. I sat within his visual field, next to him, caressing his hands gently, only smiling when he looked at me. No life experience would have been helpful at a time like this. I did what I would have wished him to do for me under similar circumstances—be gently physically connected, left in peace to do what I needed to do in silence.

"The doctor arrived at noon, as arranged. He took a seat at the dining room table and began opening each of the hundred pills, pouring the powder inside into the bottom of a glass. He had previously told us about this part of the procedure, so we were prepared. After about thirty minutes, he was ready to add two ounces of water to the powder—provided Carlos was ready to drink the concoction within two minutes. He had discussed this part, too; it was expected and agreed to. Then the doctor added: 'The water combined with the powder becomes thick and is difficult to drink. Carlos will have to drink it fast; if he does not consume all of it, he will not die. He could wake up with a damaged brain; it's unpredictable what his clinical picture would be like.' As he was saying the words I was detaching—not wanting to believe what I was hearing. I didn't remember being told this part. This didn't feel okay!"

I search for Dr. Novelli's eyes, looking for something secure. I find his comforting, empathic expression.

"Maybe he had told us, but I did not remember. People signing up for death probably don't register everything that is said. I had contacted the doctor several times over the phone; he had made himself very available during the waiting period. Each time he reminded me that Carlos had to be able to drink from a cup and pass a mental examination on the day of the procedure. I didn't remember us talking about the fact that if the substance was not consumed within the time allowed, he could wake up as a vegetable. Could I have looked for something other than Seconal, something without the risk of leaving him disabled if he could not drink it fast enough?

"I remember that after his death, I learned that nothing better existed. I had so many questions. The end of *his* life, of *our* marriage, was so immediate. So irreversible. We were at the naked end."

"Despite your doubts about what could or could not have been done," Dr. Novelli tells me, "perhaps this was the right way for Carlos. How do you see this, Beatriz?"

"I have no doubt he would have chosen to enter coma in two minutes, even if he had known the risks that Vera and I had just learned."

6. I Carry a Horror in My Heart

I look at Dr. Novelli for a couple of minutes. He gestures with his hand to go on, but I continue to take my time, stewing in the anger I felt at the doctor as he sat there at our dining room table. To stall, I drink from my bottled water; I move around in my seat. I take a deep breath.

"I went back to the bedroom to tell Carlos and Vera what the doctor had just told me. Carlos said he was ready to drink the mixture. Vera and I looked at each other, meaning: 'There is no going back at this point.'"

I tell Dr. Novelli I need to go inside myself again. I feel pressure on my chest. I feel I don't have enough air. He nods, meaning he understands, and he feels okay about my going about it any way I can. The same as on that day, I am not crying in the session. The same as on that day, I am making myself strong to tell the end of Carlos' *vía crucis* today.

"Dr. Novelli," I said as a warning, "the horror part is coming next.

"Carlos took a few sips of the slushy mixture, shook his head with disgust and said: 'This is so bitter! Ask the doctor to mix it with something sweet.' I run to the dining room and ask. The doctor explained he couldn't: 'The effects will no longer be predictable.' Carlos was having a hard time drinking the thick substance from the cup. He asked for a straw. I ran to the kitchen and brought him one immediately. Vera and I exchanged looks; we could only think we were losing minutes! In panic, we started begging Carlos to ingest the lethal stuff as fast as he could. 'Another drink, Dad!'—'Carlos, love, I know how awful it tastes, but try to take another sip. Good. Another one. Please.'—'Please.'— 'Please.'—'We have only one minute left, Dad, get two more sips down, Dad!'—'Carlos, please.'

"This is the horror I carry in my heart.

"He was not quite done, when his head collapsed sideways on my recliner. Was this the coma state? Vera and I looked at each other, frightened; we saw Carlos did not get to drink all the stuff. What if he did not drink enough? We held our breath until the doctor examined how much was left: 'It is enough, he drank enough.' Vera and I looked at each other again—in great relief.

"We felt relief because he drank enough of the bitter glass.

"We felt relief because he died.

"We were expecting a drug that would help Carlos go to sleep and gradually die in his sleep. Instead, he underwent this procedure. It was obviously unpleasant for him. But it was done. As our professional nurse granddaughter said, 'Dying can really drag on for an obscene amount of time.' The death Carlos and I chose for him kept him alert to his surroundings and responsive to us until his life was suddenly turned off by the intake of Seconal. He was alive before he entered death. I am grateful that he didn't have to hang on by a thread, breathing one raspy breath at a time until his final one. And he went through it without wavering over his decision and without regret. I had to remind myself that his usual suffering was worse—that being alive for another day would have felt tragic to him. I had to remind myself that assisted death was far more traumatic for us than for Carlos, that there were two bitter minutes for him, and that's what mattered. Those two minutes set him free. They will always be a lifelong trauma for me, and this should not matter. What mattered was that he was liberated from pain that felt as horrible as 'knife stabbings into my back.'

"This thought was my only comfort, after we stood there over the recliner imploring him to swallow the lethal dose.

"The doctor examined his body several times during the next hour. Each time he respectfully asked for permission: 'Sir, I am sorry to bother you, but I need to take your vitals.' Asking permission of a dead person is sound medical practice, yet this added another touch of the surreal to the moment. He pronounced Carlos dead and was ready to leave. For his last duty, he asked me at what time I wanted the funeral home to come for the body. In five hours, I said. I did not want Carlos to accidentally wake up somewhere away from home. I also wanted Carlos to linger at home with Vera and me, just the three of us, as when we had started our family.

"Vera and I were still standing.

"We were two darn strong women.

"I wasn't done caressing him, sliding my fingers through his blond grayish hair, when Vera, trying to help, reminded me that he was no longer there, that this was the body where he lived. That did not stop me from liking to touch him whether 'he' was there or not. His face and body stayed warm for some time, according to my sensations, despite what I had read—they say people get cold the moment their heart stops beating. His warmth was real to me; it was a bitter elixir.

"Vera was in full executive mode, attending to funeral arrangements and focusing on what needed to be done. With a lot on her plate, she kept me on her radar.

" 'Mom, it will be best if you leave the bedroom now. There are two women here from the funeral home; they have to transfer Dad from the recliner to a stretcher. They assured me they would move Dad very, very gently.'

"I wanted Carlos to be handled with the utmost care. So I went out to the living room reluctantly, wondering how two women could manage to move his stiff body—six feet, four inches tall—'very gently.' Logic said that Carlos would not suffer any discomfort four hours after he had been pronounced dead. Nevertheless, part of me wanted to stay in there and protect him, just in case.... During those hours when he remained at home, the distinction between *alive* and *dead* wasn't that clear to me. Blurriness felt comfortable—because it didn't seem real. When I think about that day, I still prefer to see it blurry. The blurrier the better.

"I never looked at their faces, but remember the dark suits of the two women. When they were done, Vera came out to the living room to get me.

" 'Mom, you can come now to say the last goodbye to Dad.'

"I went back to the bedroom and stroked Carlos' hands, the hands that had cared for me in health and in sickness, the only hands I trusted to give me injections until I was in my forties, the hands I loved, the hands I will always love. I was groping him in the stretcher.

"Vera came back and said that the women were ready to wheel him away.

"I did not want to hear those words! I embraced Carlos' body. And I yelled! And yelled! I didn't recognize the screams as mine. I had never sounded like an animal howling in misery. Who knows what I said. All I thought was that Carlos would vanish forever in seconds, and that there was nothing I could do to stop that.

" 'Mom, it would be best if you stay inside the apartment; the stretcher will have to be placed in the elevator in a vertical position, and you...'

"Vera thought the sight would be too much for me to bear. She was right. She proposed that we go together in another elevator and meet the stretcher and the women downstairs. We did. They loaded him into a black transfer van and drove him away and disappeared in the vast and misty darkness of the night. Is vast darkness the habitat of death? Is death an infinite dark night?

"I was grateful that Vera was with me. That she was the one holding me at the very moment that my life was exploding into a million pieces. Never had I lived through such helplessness. Protected by her arm around me, we went back upstairs in very slow motion. I repeated to myself:

"He won't be here tonight to kiss goodnight....

"We will not have our bear hug in the morning....

"This world will be sad without his sunny smile."

"This was the end of my life, as I had known it. Everything has changed ever since. Only my love for Carlos has remained intact. I loved him in life, and I love him as much in death. Our shared love story ended that day. It is gone from the world, but it continues inside my heart."

I look up at Dr. Novelli, and I see him looking back at me. I am grateful to have him listening, containing me as I recount the worst day of my life. And suddenly I feel a gratitude wash over me—for that doctor unscrewing the pills at our dining room table, and making sure Carlos drank down the medicine properly, and calling the funeral home. There are not many doctors who will do that job, and without them, people would not find their way out of suffering. I am still feeling traumatized, but reliving that day and my personal horror makes me recognize the good amid all the bad—and helps me see the bad that much more clearly. The slight awakening rides with me down the elevator and out into the darkening street.

7

Dancing Interrupted

Not even my morning companions, the doves in courtship, have bothered to visit me today. I miss how they show off as they dance around each other and do funny shimmy-shake moves. They bring a raw instinctual energy to my windowsill. They are not here today—flying in the rain might not be their thing.

The gray skies are an instant trigger of nostalgia. Their damp grayness gets me musing about Gustavo. Our companionship started out colorful, full of laughter and fun projects. I don't want to get sad so early in the day....

I lie down on the white living room sofa that accommodates my entire five-foot, six-inch body, and position its small red pillows under my head, close my eyes, and open an inner scenario where my musings can play. The small red pillow evokes my mother's industrious hands gifting me a pink embroidery pillow "to daydream about Carlos" when I began dating him. I had forgotten her caring gesture up until this red pillow reminded me of her. Today, December 1, would have been the 116th birthday of *mi querido papi* (my dear dad). I am going to celebrate it by writing him a note:

You were the sun of my childhood. You shone even at night. I still remember the moment when the noise of the black wrought-iron door announced your coming back from work. I ran as fast as I could down the long corridor, raising my arms as I came near you. Swiftly, you picked me up and carried me on your chest. Mom used to give us a disapproving glance and say: "She is too old for that." She probably felt left out of our perfect duet.

If there is an otherworld, I would like to think you and Carlos would have seen each other by now. The same illness that killed you took him away. I know how much you loved each other. He had to leave me a year ago, and I had no choice but to let him go. I am having a hard time with the "forever" part of dying.

"Don't Be Sad When I'm Gone"

Whenever I hurt, I remember the time you made me look away when a mother was spanking her child in the street. I was five and her child must have been two. That day and all days of my childhood you protected me from seeing the darker side of life. But you couldn't have shielded me from Carlos' death. Ah—how much I desire to have him back.

The unconditional love you gave was like an extra sense; I had to choose Carlos, a man as generous, patient and protective as you were.

Dad, I love you for being the guardian angel of my life. I so miss your tenderness.

Beatriz.

Young father Bernardo and child Beatriz recover their chronological ages when Carlos joins them in a celebratory embrace. I love and miss both of them *in the present time*—refusing to use the past tense just because they aren't here anymore.

Coming back to reality in the living room, I notice the drizzle is still sifting down persistently. With this fitting backdrop for nostalgia I've thought of Carlos and of Bernardo; of the recent tension with Gustavo; of the doves absent from my window. I feel lonely, discolored as Buenos Aires is today, gray as the skies of Portland in the fall.

Oops—it's almost therapy time! I stop my visit with the two most important men in my life, admiring them for spreading love around just being who they are. I rush out of the apartment, but on the way to Dr. Novelli's office I notice both of them are still with me. At the corner of Posadas and Callao, I lift my arms towards the sky, set Carlos and Bernardo free, and watch them fly away as white doves.

A phrase comes to me from nowhere: "Carlos and my tango..." I will save these words for my session—they may harbor a revelation.

The front door unlocks, and I notice how often I feel absorbed into my inner world when I enter Dr. Novelli's building. I am a Pavlovian dog that, instead of salivating at the sight of food, gets *ensimismada* when entering this lobby. *Ensimismamiento*—a term with no English translation that means being completely lost in thought—is an apt preparation for the introspective therapy I am doing. The elevator ride to the third floor and the ringing of office 34 happen without my willful participation.

I am ready to start my session, but the words I had saved for Dr.

7. Dancing Interrupted

Novelli have vanished—have gone away like Carlos, like Bernardo, like cordiality with Gustavo, like the doves from my window. Silently I wait for the words to come back.

Dr. Novelli: "What are you thinking about, Beatriz?"

"I am trying to recall words that came to me this morning. I have them now: 'Carlos and my tango.' I am intrigued by how these words require my attention. Are they a commentary about how Carlos encouraged my dancing? Do they capture our marriage as a dance of mutual attention and connection?"

I pause: the incomplete thought "Carlos and my tango" brings up pictures in which Carlos, me, and tango are all intertwined.

"He definitely encouraged my tango. He persuaded me to take more and more dance lessons, suggested I travel to other communities to dance, and encouraged me to go to Buenos Aires to study among its very roots. He was as achievement-oriented with my dance as he was with his medical projects. Sometimes he could be a bit overwhelming with his 'helpful' ideas. About nine years ago, realizing I was interested in the worldwide presence of tango, he persuaded me to write a book, convincing me that I was the right bicultural person, with the appropriate psycho-anthropological background for the project. I rejected the idea—just because sometimes I acted contrarian in response to his helpful ideas. I experienced them as expectations. However, my heart smiled when I heard his suggestion, after I had rejected the idea! Neither of us knew the time commitment we were making. My long writing hours made him a writer's widower for the best part of six years. He deprived himself of my full attention for all those years. He was definitely a saint—and so was my father Bernardo who is ever-present today. My book was dedicated 'To Carlos, for his infinite patience and unfailing support.' After it was published, he did not hide how proud he was—he made sure to carry the book's fliers to pass around when he thought appropriate. Tango was 'our thing' in this sense, even if it really was 'my thing'—I had authored the book, and I was the dancer.

"When he was weak and opted to drive less, he supported my tango. When I preferred to stay home rather than going out, he would recite like a catechism the emotional and physical benefits of dancing. If his advice didn't mobilize me, my persistent Carlos would redouble his efforts by making bigger offers such as driving me and picking me up. I accepted when he was having a better evening—I knew that driving me would give him pleasure. To negotiate the return, I called him to assess how he was feeling, and either waited for him or hailed a taxi."

I pause a bit, feeling teary-eyed about his kindness.

"After Carlos' passing, tango became my royal road to healing, my way to mourn while in a tango embrace with friends. How would I have coped without the music, the lyrics, the utterly humane embrace? It would have been close to impossible to be where I am today. I know that. Dancing was an integral part of my life and it became part of my way of grieving."

Dr. Novelli asks me, "How and when did you go back to dancing after Carlos died?"

"Soon," I say. "Many people may think it was 'too soon.' Carlos' last advice set me free to do what I liked. You remember the advice, don't you, Dr. Novelli?"

"'Don't forget to do *only* what makes you happy after I am gone.'"

"Yes. Despite his advice, though, I didn't feel any desire to go dancing in the beginning. Loud music bothered me; people bothered me too. All I wanted was to be with Carlos and for that I had to be at home in privacy and in silence, where he was omnipresent.

"A friend from the tango community, Nat, made himself present during my first days alone. He sent me messages from day one, keeping me company. He said he wanted to cook me breakfast on the weekend, and surprised me by coming with fresh eggs from his chickens, and organic potatoes, onions, and kale from his garden—and his very own cast-iron pan. He settled in the kitchen and cooked an elaborate frittata without following a recipe while conversing with me—much later I learned he was a sophisticated chef. Nat talked about my imminent return to the weekly dances, but I didn't feel like going—not during week one. I didn't feel like going the following week either. The third week, when we were done eating breakfast, he brought up the subject again, this time with an offer I couldn't refuse—'If you feel hesitant dancing with others, I would dance a couple of sets with you.' I immediately said yes—I felt protected—I trusted him like I trusted Carlos and Bernardo. So the first time I went dancing, it was under Nat's wings. He was the DJ that night, and at one point he walked me to the dance floor before the music began to play. When I heard it come on, my heart melted at the voice of Alberto Podestá while I was tango-embraced with Nat—he knew that my connection with this particular singer would fill me with joy. I had gotten to know him while working on my tango book; he sang with the big tango bands in the 1940s. The thunder I felt at that precise moment resurrected tango as an unquestionable and essential part of my life again. The triage—Carlos, Nat, Podestá—gave me a powerful shot of life at the saddest moment in my life."

I look up to engage Dr. Novelli's eyes. He is totally concentrated on me, quiet, so I say: "During my first tango outing under my friend's wings, I also felt comfortable dancing with other friends, and over subsequent weeks, I gradually felt at peace dancing with people I didn't know. I knew Carlos would be happy if he could see me dancing through my loss of him with friends and strangers. He understood what tango was about.

"The all of tango—the music, the dance, the poetry—filtered into my flesh and spoke to me more than ever before. My emotional life was in C minor, and the tango poets were my partners in grief. With them I wallowed in gray nostalgia and longings for my lost lover."

I look to Dr. Novelli again. I trust his eyes—he has been good to me. I have always approached men assuming them to be trustworthy until they prove not to be. Bernardo built my foundation of trust, Carlos never betrayed it.

"In a paragraph of my tango book," I tell him, "I encouraged readers to pursue dance as a path to grieving. I wrote that tango is so respectful of the human condition that no one would be offended if it were danced at a funeral. I could not have written any advice more fitting for myself at this time in my life. But I am not applying my own advice to myself, Dr. Novelli. I have felt fine going to dances for about two months since I arrived in Buenos Aires—but now I fight going."

I need to regroup inside, in silence for a few moments. As I open my mind to associations, the faces of two dance predators appear and I feel very angry at them.

"Dr. Novelli, I became very disturbed at dances when two men, on two different occasions and at two different venues, criticized my dancing and proceeded to offer themselves as teachers for hire. It was clear they were predators wanting to sell their phony services. As dancers, they were nothing special. But I find it hard to believe that their put-downs eroded my self-confidence in dancing. I wish I had gotten angry at them, rather than feeling bad about myself."

"What comes to mind about this, Beatriz?"

"First," I answer, "I am glad to finally get angry at them now. Other than that, I don't find a reason for avoiding dances. I am appalled that after twenty years of dancing, I am questioning its value, here in Buenos Aires of all places, the world capital of tango. People flock here from all over the world to dance—and I come here to avoid dancing. I consider this a symptom. I don't want to lose tango. I want to keep it in my life."

Dr. Novelli chuckles and prods me: "Tell me the details of the 'symptom.'"

"I have enjoyed dancing tango, researching its history, and writing about it. Now I might get dressed up and not go out, or go to a movie instead. If I do go dancing, I get impatient if I dance with mediocre partners. I feel frustrated and get a sour attitude. I get through it by distracting myself with attention to my dance posture. Is my position good? Okay. Is my core engaged? Okay. Is my head upright? Okay. Are my shoulders relaxed? Yes.

"I laugh nervously, but it has become a rather cynical routine. Somehow it balances a certain resistance I feel toward dancers in Buenos Aires—but I'm just talking to myself. I don't understand this change in me. I want to avoid dances."

Dr. Novelli smiles a little and says: "You were telling me about your 'symptom.'"

"Yes, yes, going back to my symptom. Last week I went dancing at a venue I enjoyed in past years. I only stayed for forty-five minutes. I felt disconnected with the dancers at my table, so I left. That was Sunday night. Thinking that I should go back dancing after that last night—lest I never dance again—I attended a Monday dance. I danced four sets with minimum enjoyment. I also felt anxious but, before leaving, I had a conversation with Carlos. He told me: 'You haven't been in Buenos Aires that long yet; this is a time when nobody knows you. This happens every year. You know men won't invite you until they see you dance. Remember you solved this frustration in the past by attending the same dance every week until the regulars got to know you and asked you to dance.' I felt relaxed after talking with Carlos and went home feeling okay.

"But I don't follow Carlos' advice. Something detains me from attending the same dances every week. I want to avoid dances.

"So, Dr. Novelli," I conclude, "after two-plus months here, I have lost enthusiasm about my passion of twenty years. As a matter of fact, I am distancing myself from the writing I've started as well. As if a deep hurt embitters me and engenders a generalized angry rejection."

Dr. Novelli asks, "How were the moments after you came back home from dancing when Carlos was alive?"

This question surprises the patient in me ... and it doesn't surprise the therapist in me. It doesn't because I talked about Carlos earlier on—Dr. Novelli's question is trying to lead me back to Carlos. I smile and engage Dr. Novelli's eyes. He is not about to answer questions. He is making room for me to dance my way around the session, and for that, he is keeping silent.

"What happened was quite funny," I tell Dr. Novelli. "When I came home, he stopped whatever he was doing, looked up at me, and asked: *'Hola amor, bailaste esta noche?'* (Hello love, did you dance tonight?) If I responded, 'Yes,' he was pleased and would say something like, 'Oh, that makes me happy.' If I said, 'Not as much as I wanted,' he would get up from his recliner, hold my hand and walk with me to a well-lit place, saying: 'Let me look at you in the light.' He looked me up and down, as a guy would look at a woman in the streets of Buenos Aires, and said: 'You look beautiful. I don't understand how you could manage to avoid dancing all night long.'"

I smile, enjoying how delightful Carlos was when we did this routine. Smiling too, Dr. Novelli joins me in a light exchange. "It is a cute story," I say, "but Carlos and I did not laugh. Tango is a serious dance—people don't smile when they dance. You know, the phrase that came to me this morning, 'Carlos and my tango,' is finding yet another meaning: *these were the times he and I tangoed without dancing.*

"Dr. Novelli, Carlos' routine did wonders to restore my confidence."

"You felt happy when he said those things to you," he says with empathy.

"Yes," I confess, a bit embarrassed. "Carlos saw me as beautiful and he would tell me so, up until the last days of his life."

Dr. Novelli shifts himself in the hold of his chair; he may be about to speak.

"Something is eluding us about your rejection of dancing. You returned to dancing comfortably in Portland, after Carlos' death, even though he wasn't there for your 'last tango of the evening.'"

Dr. Novelli and I are synchronized; we both feel we are missing an important link that would clarify my symptom. I am now comparing men in Portland's dances and the men in Buenos Aires and.... Voilà! The *something* comes to me now. How could I have missed this?

"Dr. Novelli," I announce, "the obvious that has eluded us has just become clear through my association. I find the *machismo* at dances in Buenos Aires ... unbearable. I don't feel *machismo* in Portland. Furthermore, what is unique to Buenos Aires is that men look at women in the eyes. When she meets the man's eyes and holds his gaze, she means, 'I am willing to dance with you'; at this moment the man completes his invitation by inclining his head toward the dance floor. In Buenos Aires I find myself stuck in this zone of gaze-engagement that goes nowhere—it fails to invite."

I realize that I inadvertently left something out of the invitation ceremony, an unconscious omission. Dr. Novelli didn't catch it because he is not a dancer.

"The woman who wants to dance ... smiles. But I don't smile. I probably look angry. I am sure I look angry. What is going on with me?"

In my musings, I am reviewing my growing anger at the dances in Buenos Aires during the past two months. Only this year am I so intolerant of their *machismo,* and it has occurred only recently, not when I first arrived here. My friend Gustavo's face appears amid these thoughts. As I glance at my watch, I see the session will soon be over.

"Dr. Novelli, guess who is on my mind at this very moment? Gustavo. We are not getting along. Our brief summertime turned tempestuous. We don't have time to go into the details today. He *is* with me—then he *is not* with me—he comes back, we have a truce—he *is* with me again—then he *is not* with me.... We've been doing this for several weeks."

Time is up and the session has to stop. Before getting up, Dr. Novelli says: "You are on to something important, Beatriz."

7. Dancing Interrupted

"I know," I respond, "it's so important that I've been blind to it for the last twenty minutes of the session."

We shake hands as usual.

Today the elevator functions as an extension of Dr. Novelli's office. I resume my session there, reflecting that sometimes, as therapy traces a symptom to its cause, analyst and patient dance to the same music. Today my unconscious was dancing hide and seek, leading astray Dr. Novelli's uncovering work. The method of psychoanalytic therapy hinges on bringing into the patient's awareness something which has lain unconscious.

I feel lightened, sensing that my aversion to dancing may not be a problem with tango at all. And from here in the elevator, as it descends to street level again, I realize I do not know if the drizzle outside continues—I don't remember looking out the window during the session. I set my hand over the mini umbrella in my purse, and know I will find out soon enough.

Sigh.

Smile.

8

Minotaurs in the Labyrinth

My voice is different today. It's powered by anger.

I silenced myself for three years while I was taking care of Carlos. I shut my voice out during my first year of mourning, when my heart was filled with loss and I faced the challenge of how to transform myself. Now I am ready to unleash years of indignation. My anger remains huge and it is specifically directed at wrongdoers—real Minotaurs in the labyrinth of modern medicine. In the labyrinth we also encountered angels.

Today I am drinking the morning caffeine at home, from an instant brew in my travel kit, as I sit at the dining room table surrounded by logs, hospital charts, and old correspondence with relatives. I am under a compulsion to refresh facts, dates, names of culprits and of benefactors—even if these details won't matter in my session. I feel my blood pressure rise, my jaws clench, my chest about to explode just by looking at what's on my table.

Carlos was a passionate physician; I watched his love of medicine blossom soon after his graduation from medical school. He first began practicing at a clinic in a remote area of Buenos Aires, accepting chickens and eggs as payment for his services. His love of medicine stayed with him through thick and thin. I admired the medical profession because I saw it through his eyes. As an academic, he valued the cutting-edge university systems where he was trained and worked throughout his career in the United States: the Chicago Medical School, Georgetown University, Johns Hopkins University, and the University of Kansas. When it was his turn for treatment, we entered the labyrinth expecting to receive good care.

8. Minotaurs in the Labyrinth

I have monovision this morning: all I can see is the harm inflicted on him by the doctors at the hospital.

Needing a real coffee, I go to Dos Escudos on my way to Dr. Novelli's office. Since I unburied this labyrinth at 6 a.m. it has been gnashing at me. I drink a macchiato standing up at the counter. I dash out to start the walk to my session. Ordinarily, Alvear Avenue is a street I thoroughly enjoy—except I can't enjoy it today. I can only see the blurred face of the oncologist who was most harmful to Carlos: I don't want to remember his face clearly, I don't want to remember his name. I can tolerate remembering the tag on his white uniform that identified him as a member of the oncology staff. My anger darkens into a hatred I am not used to feeling. But I don't mind that today.

Focused entirely on my remembered antagonists as I walk, I find myself standing in front of Dr. Novelli, who has opened the door. I usually like to smile when I first see him, but today I walk into his office hardly able to budge the set expression on my face.

"Dr. Novelli, what I need to talk about now is as hard as talking about the day Carlos died. I know all the things that happened, but knowing does not diminish their weight on my shoulders. Telling them to you would put them on a different plane. I never talked about this with anybody, so the wrongdoers escaped observation. You will be their first witness. Since I can get lost spouting ugliness, my challenge today is to talk about what Carlos suffered—not from his cancer, but from the neglect and callousness of those who treated him. Please don't let me get sidetracked by talking about medical deficiencies that most of us know.

"What we expected from the system, I realize, was old fashioned. The systems were better before they were taken over by the greed of Wall Street. Our view of the academic hospital was knocked upside down when Carlos became a patient. To say I was—and am—angry and appalled at the hospital doesn't sufficiently describe it. I felt and I feel moral indignation—still flaming. If what we have experienced is a universal occurrence, oncological departments are getting away with murder. I saw malpractice in action, malpractice executed with indifference. The oncological department was toxic for human beings.

"I have asked: Why the harm? Why the callousness? I can think of only one reason. Oncological patients are too weak to fight, and will inexorably exit the system by death."

Dr. Novelli raises his eyebrows.

"Yes, in the legally contentious United States, patients in relatively good health would not have tolerated what we put up with. This chilling thought led me to some research in the medical journals. What I found supported my disturbing assumption: only 4 percent of oncological patients sue their physicians. That is compared to 15 percent of internal medicine patients, who are more put together. By the way, you might be interested to hear that the psychiatric and the oncological patients are among the ones that sue the least. They are both groups that can't fight back. Well, I am not talking about Argentina; I don't know how things are here.

"Before I go into the nitty-gritty details of wrongdoing, I want to talk about our best experience. It will probably help me cool off. Carlos' *via crucis* with cancer started in April 2015, when we had just arrived in Buenos Aires for a four-month visit. After falling on a treacherous sidewalk—you and I both know the craters of our Buenos Aires sidewalks—he went to a hospital for x-rays. He was diagnosed with two broken ribs as a consequence of the fall, and they found a lung tumor suspected to be malignant that had grown while Carlos was asymptomatic. We packed up everything we had just unpacked, turned around, and flew back to Houston for surgery, where physician friends helped us get an emergency appointment with the head surgeon of the MD Anderson Cancer Center.

"It was the number-one ranked cancer care center in the United States, and it met all our expectations of medical excellence and humanity. Carlos was assigned to the surgeon he wanted, Dr. Garret—an empathic Canadian man. He and Carlos enjoyed warm and relaxed chats—ranging from medical matters to the great variety of Argentine Malbec wines. Carlos underwent extensive lung surgery under his expert hands. In addition to the two ribs which were broken from the fall in Buenos Aires, Dr. Garret had to break two more ribs to remove the unusually located tumor. We felt fortunate to be in his care. Dr. Garret came daily or twice a day to do inpatient rounds and check on Carlos. The postsurgical nursing stuff showed him tenderness while his pain came under control.

"It took Carlos several weeks to be completely recovered. He was released to the hotel connected with MD Anderson, where we stayed for several additional weeks. He was told he could go home later, when *he* was ready—not when the doctor, or the hospital, or the insurance company were ready. Dr. Garret assured him that the four-hour flight home would be manageable. He was correct: despite extensive surgery, a twelve-inch scar, and four broken ribs, the flight was a breeze. We felt gratitude for all the admirable doctors and nurses we were leaving behind, and for the employees we had encountered in hallways, elevators, and cafeterias, and even during housekeeping. They were trained and expected to be kind without exception, and always ready to help. This was an extraordinary feat considering the size of the place and the number of patients that pass through it.

"I wished we had stayed there, Dr. Novelli. But we couldn't remain in such a perfect cocoon so far away from home.

"Once back home, we assumed that the medical care somewhat closer to our area would be top-notch. We were wrong. We assumed it would have a humane environment. We were wrong. The department's employees with whom we came in contact had no empathy at all.

"It was here that I watched the oncologist harm Carlos physically and psychologically. During late 2015, he prescribed a dose of chemotherapy greater than necessary. This was the first of two times he failed his Hippocratic oath: *First, do no harm.* We were prepared for the typical side effects of chemotherapy—but not for an overdose of it. Carlos developed nasty side effects: pain in areas that were pain-free before, neuropathy (anesthesia) of the feet and legs that impaired his ability to walk and his balance. He had to use a cane for the first time in his life. When I would get close to his eyes, I felt he wasn't there—I fretted. Would he come back? His spirit did fully return—after several months, just as my hopes were vanishing.

"Right after the chemotherapy I spoke to the oncologist: he agreed he had prescribed a dose too high for Carlos. He was uncomfortable doing that, he said, but he had followed Carlos' request to receive a strong dose and get all his cancer cells killed. What was wrong with this picture? Carlos was the patient. Doctors should use their clinical judgment and do what is medically correct; he should *not* have prescribed what Carlos desired. I am sure what he did has a legal name. I still feel indignant about the cost exacted on Carlos for this doctor's negligence. Like many other patients and families consumed by facing these issues of life and death, we did nothing. We couldn't afford to spend any energy on fighting that would lead nowhere in the short term.

"Dr. Novelli, I don't know if there are patients' advocates in Buenos Aires hospitals. In the United States, they are usually just relatives who keep a watchful eye over how their loved ones are treated. They speak up when care is less than desirable. I was determined to be a strong advocate, and to protect my husband from further harm during his treatment. The MD Anderson Cancer Center taught me what good care was—there they literally inform families about patients' rights—and showed us what to expect from a good institution. This later hospital reduced my advocacy to a travesty. Looking back, I see now that my goal of protecting Carlos was unrealistic. It proved impossible to predict when harm was on its way.

"In late 2015, as if lung cancer had not been enough of an attack to his body, Carlos was diagnosed with a benign lumbar spinal tumor and was advised to have it removed. Carlos was taking care of his life and needs on his own at that time, moving independently.

"A surgeon in Houston was recommended as the best technician with more than twenty years of experience. He was late visiting Carlos for a follow-up on the first day of surgery. When he did come around 9 p.m., he spoke to Carlos from the door frame—he was in a rush. He ignored my questions; he didn't look at me when I addressed him. The following day he bullied us out of the hospital, claiming our insurance wouldn't pay for more days of inpatient recovery.

"A week after discharge, we went to his office for a follow-up examination. The doctor said Carlos was good to fly home. We found out too late—during the flight—that Carlos shouldn't have flown.

"During the flight, Carlos could not sit still and needed to get up every five minutes, unable to tolerate his lumbar pain while seated. Getting up, walking to the bathroom, staying inside, coming out, sitting down. He couldn't listen. He couldn't say anything. He was moving in silence. One thing consumed his mind—unbearable pain. I could tell he had reached the limits of his pain tolerance. His agitation, which he kept so poorly under control, was so intense that I feared he would have a breakdown from the combination of stress, pain, tension, and being in a confined space without the possibility of exiting. To this day, I don't comprehend how he didn't collapse during that flight while the plane was in the air.

"He did collapse upon arrival in Portland. His life was drained out of him, his resilience gone. Carlos couldn't walk at the airport. He suggested we call an ambulance and go to the emergency room.

"Carlos spent the last two years of his life in additional, unnecessary, searing pain because he was prematurely discharged to a four-hour flight.

"Dr. Novelli, I need to rant—not about opioids, since we know how they work—but about the ignorance of physicians in prescribing and managing them." I stop and look at Dr. Novelli's eyes.

"The more ranting, the better, Beatriz," he tells me with approval.

"After that nightmarish flight, Carlos was hospitalized in the internal medicine ward of another hospital. The bedside manners of the attending physicians were impeccable: they showed interest in Carlos, and they communicated with him and with me about his treatment. For once, I felt relieved from having to protect Carlos from harmful doctors. My relief was short lived. Despite their attentions, he was becoming delusional for the first time. At his bedside, I entertained the possibility that opiates were the culprit, when he woke up saying he was in a hurry to get to an auditorium—a large number of doctors were following him—asking him to lecture. In real life, Carlos frequently lectured to physicians on the proper use of medications. I asked him if it could have been a dream that he just had. He replied that it was really happening. I told him I understood and suggested that he relax—it was a delusion. As a psychologist, I could not help but view his dream as a wish to teach his doctors to better prescribe his medications: he had read his chart before he went to sleep—he always asked to read his chart. With no signs of recovery by the end of five days, he could not be discharged home, and yet our fate, as patients, dictated by Wall Street, was *'Your five days are up.'*"

I have the impression that Dr. Novelli is incredulous about what he is hearing. But he knows I am truthful.

"Carlos accepted the transfer to a rehabilitation facility where he could undergo daily personalized physical therapy to recover his lost capacity to walk. His first night there, he awoke around 3 a.m. in a state of panic, not knowing where he was. I became alarmed and wondered what variables were introduced at the rehabilitation center to cause the panic; back at the more familiar hospitals, he had no panic attacks. I put on my advocate hat and began asking about the drugs and dosages he was receiving. In this state-of-the-art facility, it took days to get a straight answer. Initially the rehabilitation center had two sets of prescriptions: the list from the hospital which Carlos got at discharge, plus a list written upon his admission by the facility's own doctor—who wasn't on site full-time. Which list were they using? Or were they administering the meds in *both* lists? I kept these questions to myself until I could locate the prescribers, to figure out together how to ameliorate his pain without altering his mind.

"I relaxed then, but kept watching. He received fewer medications but he still woke up in pain. I had a scary thought. Without my intervention, he might have received massive opioid doses during his upcoming inpatient stay, which could have brought on panic attacks in the middle of the night.

"A week before Carlos' discharge, I engaged the opinion of the palliative doctor at the Health & Science hospital, Dr. Eric, an angel that soon left the institution for Harvard Medical School. I asked him what he thought about me giving Carlos marijuana pills for two nights before his discharge from the rehabilitation center. I did not want to go home with an arsenal of opioids. He approved the plan, gave me a prescription for it, and told me where to apply to the state for a medical marijuana card. I shared the plan with Carlos, and he was for trying anything other than opioids. The plan was that instead of the medications brought to him at night, he would take the marijuana pills. He did. Carlos' response was excellent; he could sleep the whole night with two marijuana pills—they didn't affect his mind and he had no pain. My plan made a difference. He was discharged with lucidity—and without OxyContin, or oxycodone, or anything else that altered his mind.

8. *Minotaurs in the Labyrinth*

"The number of opioids he received during his inpatient stay at the hospital, as well as at the rehabilitation center, leads me to infer that when a patient is hospitalized the system is generous with pain medication, even if it causes delusions, disorientation, confusion, and panic. Why? Because patients under opioids are less bothersome. Especially at night."

I take a sip from my water. I don't need any prompting today. I am on a rampage.

"This same system that showers pain medication on inpatients becomes stingy with it for outpatients. It was during outpatient care at yet another hospital that I witnessed the medical staff degrade Carlos. They denied him pain relief to the point of cruelty. They abandoned Carlos to suffer, and placed me in the helpless predicament of not knowing how to make him comfortable at home. The physicians don't know how to treat pain and they make patients suffer because of it.

"In May 2017, Carlos began to suffer a pain whose origin no specialist could pinpoint. Two years had passed by then since his lung surgery, and more than one year had passed since the poorly managed lumbar surgery. But this new pain in 2017 was something distinct, and we had no choice but to seek outpatient care for it.

"I remember how, during a certain outpatient visit, I said to the physician's assistant assigned to us by Carlos' internist: 'Carlos is alive. As the medical doctor he is, he is telling you that the muscle relaxants you want to prescribe won't do anything for his condition. You are not treating him. You are treating your own fears.' She refused to consider other medications, so we got up and left the office, suggesting she take the muscle relaxants herself.

"Looking back, it is clear that Carlos' cancer was metastasizing at a rapid pace then and they offered him muscle relaxants. They treated him like a drug addict begging for pain pills."

I cover my mouth with my hand, feeling horrified. "Dr. Novelli, can you imagine the pain Carlos must have been under? He had metastasis in his bones, and in his liver, and they were denying him medication."

We look at each other in silence.

When I can breathe again, I say: "Carlos' medical specialty was in clinical pharmacology—he had completed his training in medications, their interactions, and side effects at Johns Hopkins. He knew more about drugs than any regular internist. Yet, in his final days, he was at the mercy of their ignorance.

"Physicians invoked their concerns about addiction to leave patients suffering. Carlos found this ideology bizarre, and so did I. Carlos would not get addicted ... but even supposing that he, as a cancer patient, somehow did get addicted to pain relief pills.... What would the problem be, exactly?

"Carlos was in atrocious pain for six months. He was passed around from physician to physician. Not one of them referred him to a palliative specialist. Any of his four doctors could have done that. The palliative doctor was part of the oncology department. Why didn't they? Negligence? Stupidity? Cruelty?

"While Carlos was abandoned to suffer, my friend Dottie in Kansas was living relatively pain-free with metastasized bone cancer. Her private neurosurgeon had implanted a pump on her back, with painkillers inside, including morphine. She was able to regulate the outflow of medication by pressing a button while going about her life as usual.

"The main culprit of Carlos' suffering was the oncologist: he was Carlos' main doctor. I hold him responsible for turning a deaf ear to our pleas. He stopped returning our messages. He sent us away and had a clerk call us instead; the message was that Carlos' pain was not cancer-related, and thus not under his specialty. He was lying—no one knew the origin of his pain in 2017. No one knew until one month before he died, when the imaging studies showed metastasis in his bones and liver. Exceptional clinical problems can be hard to diagnose; we knew that. But we also knew that pain of unknown origins can nonetheless be ameliorated by the palliative specialists.

"The oncologist failed in his Hippocratic Oath—'First, do no harm'—for the second time by failing to use good judgment and refer him to the palliative doctor in his own department. He did harm.

"The final abandonment occurred when we had an appointment to see him after the November radiological study. That day, that November 14, we found ourselves utterly defeated by the system. The oncologist told Carlos that he had metastasis in his liver and bones. He gave him four weeks to live. Four. Weeks. To live. I was speechless. Carlos, who, according to my log, had been hopeful the day before, asked: 'So what now? What can I do?'

8. *Minotaurs in the Labyrinth*

"We could contact hospice, the oncologist said, or apply for medically assisted death at home. He referred him to the palliative specialist. Six months too late, he referred him to the palliative specialist—after the insufferable had been suffered.

"On our way out of the oncologist's office, I turned around, saw the oncologist, looked him in the eye, and said: 'Why did you not refer Carlos to the palliative doctor six months ago?'

"'I should have done that. I am sorry. It did not occur to me,' he said.

"The words 'I am sorry' meant nothing to me. Doctors are trained to say 'I am sorry' when they are caught in mistakes; it has been studied that patients are less likely to sue if they hear an apology. Without a further word and looking at him with disgust, I hastened to catch up with Carlos. We held hands tightly, walked away through the toxic hallways of the oncology wing, looking down, our hearts destroyed. In silence.

"On November 14, we were given an appointment to see the palliative doctor for November 27, when Carlos would have two weeks left. With four weeks to live, he had to wait ten days for relief. If this is not madness, what is?

"On the 27th, we met Dr. Katie. The moment we saw her, we realized we had found our angel. In her pink suit and high heels, she looked youthful and lively—and proved an unexpected miracle, a combination of kindness and efficiency we had not encountered at the hospital so far. At the end of our battle, she was our godsend. It brings a smile to my face remembering her question as she examined Carlos: 'Does your tummy hurt?' It felt endearing. The three of us looked at each other smiling. She had a young child and was used to this language, she said. Realizing the pain Carlos was under, she got ready to give him an injection, which took much longer than necessary because she had to fight with the administration to let Carlos have it for immediate relief.

"The madness of the system did not have room for kind solutions.

"We liked that Dr. Katie was a warrior ready to fight for her patients. She was the first sane doctor we had encountered. We could relax now. She was logical, she made sense, she was protective—she was the doctor I had wished Carlos could have had ever since we returned from MD Anderson. As she read his chart, she learned Carlos was a clinical pharmacologist, and showed interest in his opinion about the drug she considered prescribing for him. As his whole body twisted with pain, Carlos gave his opinion: 'It is a good one, I wrote a paper on it.'

"To our relief and delight, she was the last doctor who cared for him. She could have treated him for the last six months if any of Carlos' doctors had made the referral. This is still my chagrin. Dr. Katie knew how to make a suffering patient feel comfortable without drugging him to oblivion. She made his life, our lives, bearable during his last days. As a result, Carlos' mind was clear, and we were able to communicate during our final days and hours together.

"I told her I would understand if she didn't have time to attend her patients' memorials, but I wanted to invite her to Carlos' anyway. She said she would be happy to attend. And she gave me a keepsake; she told me: 'When I saw you the first time and he was in his highest pain, I noticed how lovingly he looked at you, how he was appreciative of everything you did to help him. His eyes were filled with love for you.'

"Dr. Novelli, I've drowned you in words today. I don't know how I've kept this craziness inside for two years. The person that stuck with me through bad pain, hope, and worse, was Carlos' niece Roxana. From 5,000 miles away, she was my single sustaining support. My heart glows when I think about her," I tell Dr. Novelli with a hand on my heart.

"This session was overdue, Beatriz," says Dr. Novelli, adding: "You will feel lighter now."

I take a long pause. This is not just another therapy session. I have unloaded bricks of impotent anger which I've withheld for what seems like an eternity.

"Dr. Novelli, may the Minotaurs disappear from my memory. I hope Dr. Katie and Dr. Garret will be the only doctors that stay in my memory. I wish for the others to fade into oblivion and rest in peace. Does that sound odd to you?

"Somehow I like the idea of a quiet celebration, after finally bringing this weight to you and unburdening myself. I will go home and rest, and then head to Hotel Sofitel's restaurant. Last year, Carlos and I got a membership to the gym there, and we treated ourselves to lunch after exercising. Carlos and I were attracted by a cheerful glass sculpture there, like a Chihuly mobile, that hung across the ceiling, ten feet long with floating forms in bright blues, reds, yellows, and greens. The distant courtesy of a French hotel suits me well today; the servers remember Carlos and me from last year. I will order the *Gancia* Carlos used to like—the one I never drank for fear of getting dizzy. I will be left alone, to dine and raise a *Gancia* in his honor, wearing this new lightness on my shoulders."

9

Missteps of a Widow in the World of Singles

After a few visits to Café Francesca where the tables are always available, I have returned to Dos Escudos. I am returning to my first love, the cozy breakfast and lunch place of savory food lovingly prepared, and to its human flora.

I am carrying a small metal box in my hand with the remains of an aroma.

Before I left home this morning, a bottle of perfume Carlos gave me fell from the small shelf under the mirror and shattered on the tile—Dior's Dioressence. It is from the 1980s, and it can't be replaced. Dior is now making Dioressence under the same name but without the same original jasmine aroma. I got tearful looking at the pieces of glass on the floor. I hit the counter in frustration and soaked up the scattered drops of perfume with cotton balls to try and preserve the scent. Will the aroma last forever in a metal box?

I intend to take the box to Fueguia later, the perfume makers two blocks from here on Alvear Avenue, thinking they might be able to reproduce the aroma for me. I am staring at the box I placed next to the salt and pepper shakers on the table, when Martín, the server who is after my attention, comes over to take my order.

"Steak with mashed potatoes. Shall I get out of my comfort zone and order wine to find out if it makes me dizzy? Chardonnay, please," I say. He is conversational as usual, and expresses curiosity about the metal box with the cotton balls. I tell him I broke a perfume bottle I can't replace. He tells me he knows a lot about perfumes. "How come?" I ask. He tells me that during the twenty years he lived and worked in

Spain he learned about perfumes. This is when he very casually adds: "I will buy you a perfume you will love."

I look at him dumbfounded.

"You don't believe me, do you?" he asks. "I know where to buy perfumes, I can take you sometime soon."

I remain speechless. I manage to just smile. This server is telling a customer of the company that employs him that he will buy her a perfume—if I told the owner, he would be fired, so he is a risk taker. And he is saying he will buy me a perfume in the same tone as when he asks me what food I want to order. What is going on? I think about the ways he has tried to be noticed, and realize that he finally got the attention he could not get from me before. Up to this moment he has been a server named Martín who works alongside the sweet women servers Carlos used to befriend. I have not done what I said I was going to do—look at Martín "as a guy." I am looking at him now when he is busy and cannot see me, noticing he is skinny; a tall, Middle Eastern type, with intense black eyes; fairly good-looking, in his late thirties. He gets eight stars in looks and two stars in honesty. Two months after my coming here almost daily, he is becoming Martín "the guy" who is flirting, the one who befriended me when I first arrived in mid–September without my noticing his intentions. He had to say something outrageous, like he will buy me a perfume, for me to get it. I am a widow recently coming out of the woods. But I could be his mother. I pay another server and leave.

It's time to stop by Fueguia on the way to my session. I've seen the locale in passing countless times—a very long and narrow storefront painted and decorated in black. Today I walk inside for the first time. Its ambiance is ultra-chic, dramatic, sexy, mysterious—something out of Rodeo Drive. Small perfume bottles rise atop three-inch wood pedestals on a black tablecloth that runs the length of the store. No sales personnel are in sight. I feel free to smell aromas with intriguing names—*Alguien sueña* (Someone dreaming), *Cactus Azul Patagonia* (Patagonian blue cactus). A woman dressed in a black uniform wearing minimal makeup comes out of the back room of the store and sits at a French Louis XV style desk on the far end. She doesn't come to me—I go to her and note that her non-glamorous look is atypical of personnel who sell perfumes. I sit on a French Louis XV–style armchair to tell her my story. She informs me that Fueguia doesn't custom make aromas, but she might be able to find perfumes with similar ingredients. She fetches a book containing the formulas of all existing aromas, looks up Dioressence in my presence, confirms it was a 1980s fragrance and shows me its ingredients. Knowing the composition, she proceeds to look for similar Fueguia aromas. I smell several but, by the fourth one, my olfactory senses are so saturated that I can't differentiate them. She shows me a silver container with coffee beans that clear up the olfactory nerve endings. I alternate smelling aromas and coffee beans but feel no affinity for any of fragrances. I could take aromas home, she says, and feel free to come back as many times as I needed to sample more—all of that is said without any pushy saleswoman energy. She acts as an information provider.

Wishing I could stay longer, I have to leave this spectacular display marketed as "the essence of Argentina" with fragrances inspired by Patagonia, the grasses of the pampas, and the northern desert. I stand up to make one more round of the store's display area, and then look for the saleswoman to say goodbye before leaving. She has disappeared into the back room at the far end of the store where the laboratory is. Fueguia has elevated perfume making to an art for connoisseurs— not caring to engage in the high-pressure sales techniques used on the masses in more commercial perfumeries.

I walk to the exit door and as I open it, I discover that it has suddenly begun to pour outside. My glasses fog up at once in the summer heat and humidity. I know the sun will be out soon, unlike in Portland where the rain can last for months, but for the moment water is pounding the sidewalks.

I take a taxi to my session just four blocks away. "This is Buenos Aires," where you step outdoors, and taxis line up in front of you. Unlike in New York, they don't mind giving you a ride for just a few blocks.

During the short taxi drive to Dr. Novelli's office, I remind myself that I have an agenda: to discuss a male friend, one who is neither a new friend nor perhaps a friend at all anymore. I can hear my daughter's voice warning me soon after Carlos died: "Mom, you are going to be surprised when you meet men—they aren't like Dad. Dad was off the charts."

So far, she has been right.

9. Missteps of a Widow in the World of Singles

Before death did us part, I had always attended social events in my adult life as a married person, mostly but not always with Carlos. During my marriage I socialized with single friends and with couples. My new social life is likely to have more singles. I feel open to new friendships with men and women, but I am sure it will be an eye-opener to mingle with singles in a society that has changed while I was married. The solid ways that Carlos and I enjoyed are no longer the norm, I realize, or even desired. Today women and men in this city flaunt that they prefer sexual companions to boyfriends or girlfriends. I usually ask why. The response I get is: "You don't have to have a relationship." A single man talked to me about "polyamorous love" and its resurgence in this city. People looking for new paradigms would suffocate in the around-the-clock sharing of life that was so sweet and satisfying for Carlos and me.

I get to Dr. Novelli's office building fifteen minutes early and see the doorman sitting at the end of a console table. I ask if I could sit at the other end. He says I can, but why don't I go upstairs to the office? It is the third time I've been early and all three times he has suggested that I go upstairs: this is the third time I tell him there is no waiting room upstairs, and I need to get some work done while I wait. I open my laptop and begin to type.

After the recent session when Dr. Novelli and I discovered I was angry at the machismo of local dancers, I waited a week and returned to tango again. At one point during a night out, I took a walk to the restroom. On my way there I passed by an acquaintance, Juan Manuel, who was sitting at a table in the non-couples' area. I had met him at Hospital Borda, a psychiatric hospital, four years ago, while researching the benefits of dancing for psychotic patients; Juan Manuel was teaching the class there. We chatted after his class was over, and one of his comments remained crystal-clear in my memory: "When I come here to teach these psychotic patients to dance, I breathe a kind of humanity I don't find in the world outside these walls."

Challenging myself to break out of my safe comfort zone, on the way back from the restroom I leaned over next to him and said: "Hello, Juan Manuel, do you remember me? I am Beatriz."

"Don't Be Sad When I'm Gone"

He hesitated as he looked at me and said: "Oh, Beatriz…. Beatriz Dujovne? Yes, I remember you. You are the author." He asked where I was sitting. I said, "In hell, far away, where I blend in with the wall." He suggested I walk back to my seat, he would follow me with his eyes, so he could find me later. Then he came and invited me to dance.

Our dancing was seamless and enjoyable. He said he liked how we danced together. An affirmation from someone like him—an older self-made *tanguero,* a gentleman and an expert dancer—isn't a minor thing. We exchanged phone numbers; he said he would call me to go dancing. Two weeks later, we arranged to go to a dance hall called El Beso. We sat together, which in Buenos Aires is a tacit agreement to dance with one another exclusively. He was such a good partner that I danced floating a couple of millimeters above the dance floor. I was worried about dancing exclusively with him and felt an urge to go home after one hour—odd behavior on my part, knowing it had taken him more than an hour to meet me there. All the same, he offered to come out with me, and accompany me to a taxi, but I said I preferred to leave by myself.

After this outing, we went out again to a dance starting at 11:30 p.m. We sat in the row of small tables along the wall, all covered by bright yellow tablecloths, where couples got seated. Juan Manuel told me to let him know when I wanted to dance, since he would love to dance every single set. We continued to dance: floating above the wooden floor with him was becoming addictive. I didn't feel the urge to leave this second time. At 1:30 a.m. we were saying goodbye at the door when he suggested I should call him next time, not just to go dancing, but to go for a walk and conversation. I smiled and said I understood; however, it didn't seem like a good idea. Calling him would have indicated my interest in some type of amorous relationship—which I didn't have. I respected the person he was and had a good relationship with a common friend we discovered we had who had told him about my book. I debated between being rude or doing something I didn't feel comfortable with. Carlos' words—"Promise me you will do only what you like so you can be happy"—helped me make a decision. I didn't call to go for a walk, but I called him a month later to wish him a happy new year.

The doorman keeps reminding me to go upstairs. "Thank you," I say, but remain seated until 3:59 p.m.

Getting outside my comfort zone brought about a good outcome: I learned I can dance beautifully when I have an expert lead. Perhaps it didn't bring a good outcome for Juan Manuel—who knows?

Pondering ... pondering.... I ring Dr. Novelli's office on the third floor, where he opens the door as usual, is cordial as usual, and is casually dressed as usual. I engage his kind eyes as usual, and dash to my corner of the moss green sofa. As I find my place on the couch, I tell Dr. Novelli that I hope to understand myself through the difficult relationship I've been having with my old friend Gustavo.

"Dr. Novelli," I begin, "I would like go back to one of our recent sessions, when I was talking about my sudden aversion to dancing in Buenos Aires. Gustavo's face appeared to me as I was telling you about that."

Dr. Novelli remarks that he remembers how my easy companionship with Gustavo lasted for about four weeks before it suddenly changed for the worse.

"Exactly," I say. "For a few weeks we went to movies, had dinner together, and enjoyed long chats. We saw *The Shape of Water* and *Roma*, and enjoyed our lively discussion of the films. During one of our early dinners, we talked about him visiting Portland next year, and driving down Route 101 to San Diego, stopping at museums and architectural landmarks along the way. Our smooth ride turned rocky in late October, during a conversation we had at the Tienda del Café, the one at Santa Fe and Callao. We ordered espressos. I slid a half-typed page on the table, intending to read it to him later—he had previously shared a reading with me. When the moment felt right, I picked up my page and said, 'I brought something to share with you.' In a categorical tone, he issued an *order:* 'Don't read it. I don't want to hear it.' He was not joking. Dumbfounded, I looked at him with a poker face while he went on talking about himself. Once I recovered from the shock, I interjected in his monologue: 'How do you feel about your Hitler number?' 'Just fine,' he said, 'because that's how I feel.' His next statement blew my mind but it didn't shake my ability to talk: 'Any woman who treats me like she's my wife will be fired in two minutes.' I fired back: 'Too bad you had such experiences with wives; in my book, 'wife' means loving and caring.' He became defiant and controlling, as if he needed to exert power over me. I decided to rely on my inner strength to defy his defiance. I could tell our companionship was doomed. It has gone up and down since then; he can be excellent company one day and obnoxiously controlling the next."

Having updated Dr. Novelli, I pause, tired of hearing myself. I need to breathe. Dr. Novelli stays with my silence for a while, and then asks: "The dynamics with Gustavo—are they replicated at the dances, Beatriz? You dance when, and only when, 'he' wants you to dance. 'He' has the control. 'He' is Gustavo ordering you not to read, and 'he' is all the men at the dances that decide if you dance or if you don't get to dance."

It is my turn to listen. I nod for him to continue.

"You are resisting 'his' control at the dances. It did not bother you before, neither in Portland nor in Buenos Aires, as long as things were okay with Gustavo. It bothers you now that Gustavo became your Hitler. Your feelings at the dances are saying: 'I've had enough machismo with Gustavo, I don't want any more machismo in my life.'"

"Yes, yes, a trillion times! Your interpretation feels right on target. This completes the picture. I feel it in my gut."

"You are projecting Gustavo's face onto the *tangueros*," adds Dr. Novelli, "and displacing onto them your anger at Gustavo."

I pause to take in what Dr. Novelli said. I had such a blind spot that I could not see this dynamic by myself. I didn't want to face how toxic my friendship with Gustavo has been. I never know where we stand. I have been loyally sticking by him and his illness like I did with Carlos—but Gustavo isn't Carlos. If anything, he is the anti–Carlos. This relationship needs to end.

I resume telling the story of recent events, to see where it leads Dr. Novelli.

"Since our friction at Tienda del Cafe, our weekly outings have dwindled down to chats via Skype. You know … it was a couple weeks after Tienda del Café that I began avoiding dances. I have been letting him initiate contact, mostly hour-long conversations. He also initiated a couple daytime outings to museums. We enjoyed those. But we have only met about once a month. The off-times with Gustavo happen when I resist his attempts to control me: we can't negotiate, so we part ways."

Dr. Novelli: "His offer to you is: 'What's mine is mine, and what's yours is mine.'"

Puzzled, I ask: "Do you mean he annexes me to control me?" Dr. Novelli nods in agreement.

I pause briefly to take in these insights that make so much sense.

"Just recently he invited me to his apartment for the first time in three months. The plan was to take a walk in his neighborhood and then to go to dinner. Our walk was pleasant since there was much to admire in the 1920s houses recently updated in the neighborhood. After a ninety-minute walk, we sat down for a *merienda* of afternoon tea or coffee. Then I became the target of his aggression. I was feeling cold and wanted to leave the outdoor table, but he wanted to stay because he wasn't done talking. He made fun of me: 'Poor baby, she is cold.' The lowest blow came right after, while I was waiting for him to pay so we could leave and he was dragging his feet. 'You are used to being treated like a princess,' he chuckled; 'I am not going to treat you like a princess.' I hit him back with gusto: 'I treated him like a prince too. It is nice to be spoiled a little. Nobody will treat you like a prince with your Hitler ways.' We started to walk back to his apartment and he said I was 'getting angry for nothing.' I became furious, told him to stop talking to me, and walked fuming the rest of the way, went upstairs, picked up my purse and left. Dinner was out of the question, I said. I left thinking we had finally broken up. Never had I been a drama queen in my adult life like I was that evening.

"Well into summer, he suggested meeting at Café Babieka. Another tsunami was in store. He asked me why we were meeting. 'It was your idea,' I said; 'I came thinking we were going to figure out what part we played in that last war in your neighborhood.' Before I was done saying 'war,' he said he was not going to apologize because he had not done anything wrong. I told him, 'You were aggressive and controlling, and it is time you realize that I will *never* submit to you.' I placed my index finger close to his nose when I said *never*, I felt strong. I didn't want to linger there fighting, so I just sat there as calmly as I could, pointing out how he was devaluing me—in real time. We agreed it would be best to leave. The next day he called to find out how I felt about taking a trip to see if we could get along. His sudden shifts from cold to hot in a matter of seconds take me by surprise, although they have happened every time we are together in person. I believe it is not only me having a hard time separating from him; Gustavo has a hard time separating from me as well."

Dr. Novelli: "You see how Gustavo devalues you."

"Yes! I also see his self-centeredness, his need to overpower me—he is a control freak. All disagreements are my fault, and he is always rewriting history to make me the bad guy. He sees his capacity to turn the page after an angry outburst as a mature skill I don't have. He can talk non-stop for forty-five minutes, but he looks at his watch when I start talking. I've excused his dictatorial aspirations up to now because he lacks control over his illness, and he needs to control something—me. He has suffered a lot."

Dr. Novelli: "Beatriz, you present two facets of Gustavo. What a good companion he can be, how much you laugh together, how entertaining he can be, how creative he is. That is one facet. The other one is his volatility, control, rewriting history, and devaluation of you. The latter is his more usual side. I think you have to join his two sides together; he probably isn't that wonderful, and not that bad either."

"Why does he keep coming back? We relate as if we were a couple in a bad marriage, but we don't even hold hands."

"He keeps you engaged for some reason," notes Dr. Novelli. "What could that be?"

"To be his audience? To control me, I guess. I don't know."

"'This devaluing is part of his personality structure, Beatriz, you know that. He can't change it."

"I know that and agree with you," I reply. "But I have an old affection for my friend Gustavo from graduate school. I shouldn't dump someone I have affection for."

"Your old friend gives you his presence only if you submit," Dr. Novelli remarks, "and if you submit, you are automatically devalued."

I pause to reflect on what he said—the inequalities I had not considered before. Ouch, Dr. Novelli! You are not going to let me be in denial. You are not going to let me make excuses to stay in this bad relationship.

9. Missteps of a Widow in the World of Singles

Dr. Novelli shakes his head and asks: "What keeps you in it? In the relationship?"

"I've been asking myself the same question. I like sharing his creative work, his interesting ideas, his rebelliousness, his take on the world. Then there is more—but that 'more' eludes me."

"Could it be," Dr. Novelli proposes, "that you have stayed with him this long because you think you need a male companion in your life?"

I dwell on his question a few moments before answering.

"I want to say 'no.' But I don't feel a 'no.' Life with Carlos is all I know. Life in Buenos Aires with a friend is all I know—my old friend Celina, who died last year, was my loyal friend. Gustavo was my only old friend in Buenos Aires this year. It felt natural to let a companionship with him develop; we had a rapport from the past. Did I need a man by my side, a Carlos? Have I lingered with Gustavo for that reason? I believe it is possible."

"When you first came here," Dr. Novelli says, "you told me you didn't want to get married again. However, you may have had the unconscious expectation that you would eventually share your life with another man. Maybe not a husband—only a companion. Now that I've known you for several months as you live your life alone, never feeling bored or lonely, always engaging in projects, I see you quite able to be alone. Why don't we put it this way, Beatriz: Being alone, you can...."

"Do you mean I can ... live life?"

"Let's leave it with an ellipsis. Being alone, you can.... You have an intense relationship with your projects; in this sense you are never alone."

"Can you explain this further?" I ask.

"Your projects, such as your writing now, give back to you," Dr. Novelli answers. "You interact intensely with your writing. You may think you need someone in your life, but I know you don't."

These words are going right to my gut. They feel so true.

Since the session is just about over, Dr. Novelli adds a last comment: "It is important to connect with people who generate positive feelings in you, Beatriz."

I tell Dr. Novelli I am going inside myself for a moment to order my thoughts. I am thinking about how Gustavo and I exist for one another, outside of any *real* relationship.... I felt good with him during some of our early outings, and traumatized in later ones.... I need to take care of myself the way Carlos took care of me.... I will be leaving Buenos Aires in one month.... Calling him to say goodbye seems out of the question now.... I may contact him from the States after a reasonable hiatus to ask him about his health.... I still care about Gustavo and wish him well.... I must focus on the insight Dr. Novelli gave me....

You may think you need someone in your life, but I know that you don't.

Once out of my sanctuary, waiting for the tiny elevator, I continue reciting the precious words Dr. Novelli gave me. They will be my mantra. Deciding not to hurry but to savor the moment of clarity, I pass the elevator and go down the spiral service stairs, stepping carefully as I descend. I keep reciting down the stairs and out into the street: *You may think you need someone in your life, but I know that you don't.*

Three blocks later, still reciting my mantra, I am walking down Quintana minding my own business when I bump into Martín on the sidewalk. He is moving his motorcycle a few feet from where it is, so that he can watch it from Dos Escudos across the street. We stop, face each other and exchange *"Hola."* Quickly, he asks me: "Beatriz, have you been to La Florería?"

"I imagine that is not a flower shop. What is it?"

"It is the 'in' bar in Buenos Aires this season," he says.

"Why is it called La Florería?"

"Because it is located in the basement of a florist shop," he says. "I would like to take you there tonight. I will leave work in one hour and I could pick you up at 7 p.m."

"Where is the bar?" I ask, while I think about what to do about the invite.

"It is across 9 de Julio, in Arroyo. We can ride on my motorcycle. You will like it—they serve the best negronis there."

Needing more time to make a decision I ask him: "What's a negroni?"

"It is a popular Italian cocktail," he explains, "part gin, part semi-sweet vermouth, part Campari."

I ask him questions while I talk to myself: *Beatriz, this is an opportunity to get out of your comfort zone. You would like to take a motorcycle ride. You know Martín is a flirt, you can manage that. You also know he won't harm you. It could be a misstep—but you will grow more than if you stay home.*

"It sounds like fun. I will be outside my apartment building at 7 o'clock," I say.

Feeling brave, I go home and google La Florería. The venue sounds intriguing, it is described as the bar in vogue. It has excellent reviews in Spanish and English. I won't drink. I couldn't get on a motorcycle under my parents' watch or Carlos' watch. I know how dangerous motorcycles are, especially in the crazy traffic of Buenos Aires. I am curious about this thirty-nine-year-old inviting me out to a bar. But I feel up to the challenge.

Martín and I meet as arranged. I sit on the motorcycle; he makes sure I am comfortable; and we ride off. I realize I have no helmet exactly when we are crossing the widest avenue in the world, the nineteen lanes of 9 de Julio at the intersection with Cerrito—exactly where most traffic accidents happen. I hold on tight to his shoulders and don't worry—this is my "get out of comfort" homework. And I am *way* out. Once on the other side of 9 de Julio, we ride a couple of blocks along the quaint Arroyo Street lined by fine arts galleries and antique shops, and its grand Hotel Sofitel with its long-closed carriage entrance.

We arrive at La Florería. It is a small flower shop with exquisite flowers. Martín opens what looks like an oversized refrigerator door, asks me to wait while he goes downstairs to check the bar, and leaves the door open behind. The bar looks like a wide corridor inundated by customers standing and sitting. I am amazed that what looks like a fancy crowded subway with an unbearable level of noise has risen to be considered the "in" bar in Buenos Aires.

Martín comes back: "No room," he reports. I am happy to go elsewhere just to avoid the noise. He leads me to a charming French restaurant next door; we sit at an outdoor table and order appetizers.

He asks: "Do I have any hope?"

I question whether I really understand him and ask: "What do you mean?"

"Do I have any hope with you?" he expands. "I've been interested in you since I first saw you."

I tell him I am planning to be gone in three weeks. When he says that's okay, I totally get it: he isn't thinking beyond tonight. I realize I am being picked up by a *porteño* who doesn't beat around the bush. I move my head saying "no." He acts disappointed. Should I have gone out with him? I chuckle and tell him: "I could be your mother, you know...." He indicates he does not care about that.

"Hola, Martín!" cries an older couple passing by; they stop at our table, Martín gets up, and steps away to greet them effusively with a kiss on the check, as the three of them socialize for a moment.

I overhear that they are back from a trip to Italy and have a present for him. I am thinking this scene would never happen to me in the United States: I am having an authentic *porteña* experience where the server of the café I've patronized for months has taken me out to a bar and is trying to "pick me up" just as two patrons of the same café pass by and relieve me from turning him down. I figure that when he is done visiting with them, I will change the subject, and ask Martín to tell me about his life—I am curious about the twenty years he lived in Spain.

Before I can act on this, he comes back to the table, and tells me these clients want to be served by him. He enjoys them, and asks, "Can you give me hope?" I gesture a soft "no" and we amicably agree to leave. We climb on the motorcycle, we cross the nineteen lanes of 9 de Julio again, and he stops at my building to drop me off. I pat myself on the back for being adventurous.

He pouts and asks for a kiss. I give him a peck on the cheek. When I reach the sidewalk, I turn back to say goodbye and he is still moping.

I go upstairs slowly, and sit on the white living room sofa, feeling both exhausted and energized thinking about my days in this vibrant Buenos Aires. I don't have to look for entertainment or stimulation. Things happen to me here. They happen to everybody. I could certainly say "no" to them. But I can say "yes" and get out of my bubble. I came to Buenos Aires to say "yes" to embracing life. Even boring routines turn into experiences worth remembering.

I've gone to my gym in Portland for ten years, and never once experienced a surprise, never once made a meaningful connection or met anyone that made an impression on me. This is not a gripe; I am acclimatized to my other culture and have no interest in social surprises when I am there. I go to the gym as I go to restaurants—to do what I went to do, and leave without looking at the human landscape. But I got used to the gym in Buenos Aires pronto. My first day there, the trainer refused to shake my hand. He looked me in the eye, and with the slightest twitch at the corner of his mouth, he told me: "In Buenos Aires, we hug."

10

Playful Restorations

Most cemeteries give the impression that the buried are really dead.

Not Recoleta Cemetery—its surreal ambience may trick the mind.

Lured by pure touristic interest, I have visited this place many times before today. I've read about it, taken guided tours of it, and strolled around its grounds in search of quietude and relaxation.

In my small way, I did what those who conceived of this cemetery did on a grand scale. They created a necropolis which tempts the imagination to "sort of believe" the buried may not be totally dead. Its whimsical character compels me to visit today for a different reason—for its surreal aura. Since Carlos died, I have had many comforting experiences in this zone between reality and fantasy.

On my way to the cemetery, I walk along Quintana Avenue to my second favorite café, La Biela, where I stop to enjoy a macchiato under the sideways branches of the gigantic *ombú* tree. This colossal 400-year-old creature presides over the botanical landscaping of the sprawling park Carlos Thays. I cross the park under its building-sized branches, and through their long sweeping arms I see patches of the cemetery appearing like pieces of a puzzle. When I emerge from the precincts of the *ombú*, the cemetery gleams in full view, majestic with its grand neoclassical entrance crowned with the massive gold inscription: *Requiescant in pace* (May they rest in peace). The Latin motto along with the imposing architecture of another era—whether the Buenos Aires of the early 1900s, or the Greece and Italy of antiquity—have the power to transport the visitor outside today's reality to a past chronological time.

As I mount the oversized Carrara marble steps, and walk amid the four gigantic Doric columns to pass through the two titanic wrought-iron doors, my pilgrimage brings me into a hallway where the eyes of a life-sized Christ look directly down at me from the cross, regardless of where I am situated—like da Vinci's *Mona Lisa* at the Louvre. I have now entered this necropolis, an original miniature city planned with streets and street names at every corner, designed with spaces for green shrubs, trees, and grass—not the usual burial grounds. Like many others who come here for hauntingly inspired strolls, I can easily forget it's a cemetery and approach it as an open-air museum, crowded with mausoleums in a hodgepodge of styles—Art Deco, Art Nouveau, Neo-Gothic, Modern, and Baroque—with the best materials money could buy in Europe. In the early 1900s, Argentina was one of the five richest countries in the world, and the expert craftsmanship here shows it. The tomb façades are tastefully adorned with carvings of angels, figures of Jesus, and even stained-glass windows.

Environs for peaceful enjoyment were successfully crafted here, in this most unique of cemeteries. Elaborate windows which only the dead may look out of are the surreal hallmark of this place's design. Some of the most striking monuments rise here amid ripples of hushed rumor and phantasmagoria—and it doesn't concern me whether the stories are true or not.

I speculate that grieving families indulged in vivid fantasy as much as I did, and still do—to believe, in at least some part of the brain, that their loved ones might be worshipping, or vacationing, or just enjoying the backlit display of the stained-glass windows.

Of the 6,400 mausoleums at Recoleta Cemetery, I choose to visit two specifically: Liliana's and Rufina's, both of them laid to rest in their youth. They capture my interest this year for the first time, deeply. What their parents sought to create in these memorials seems akin to what I created in my mind after Carlos died.

The mind of Liliana Crociati's father intrigues me. He commissioned an exact replica of her bedroom, including her belongings, underground, beneath her burial site, and a life-sized bronze statue of Liliana beside a life-sized statue of her dog on the outside. This fanciful comfort *in case she wakes up* is amazing.

The tomb of Rufina Cambaceres, who died at age nineteen, was constructed of Carrara marble with a carved rose on top, and a bed carved next to it for her mother to sleep in night after night to keep her daughter company. Rufina was supposedly buried in a cataleptic state in 1902; this incident, which sent whispers of fear throughout the city of Buenos Aires, changed the funerary culture. From that day on, ringing bells were installed inside coffins, in case the dead were to wake up.

The mother sleeping close to her daughter, the placing of bells in case the deceased should awaken—these are of utmost interest to me this year. I can relate to that much better than in previous visits. What those old mourning families expressed with grandeur, I have done in minuscule with Carlos: I also engaged in many "illogical" behaviors in case he should wake up. When he ceased breathing, I kept talking and caressing his hair as usual. After he died, I insisted on keeping his body home three hours longer than required. I had the women in charge of his body promise to move him gently—to protect him, *just in case*. I have kept his closet intact, just as he left it—*in case he comes back*.

Feeling myself now in the company of those families who maintain a fantasy bond with their lost loved ones, indulging the thought that they may not be totally dead, I proceed to Dr. Novelli's office, a short walk from here.

"Good afternoon, Beatriz," Dr. Novelli greets me as he opens his door, and I am ready for my inner journey. I am so ready that as soon as I step inside his consulting room, before even sitting down, I tell him: "It is ironic. Carlos, the most consistent person in heart and action I have ever known, keeps changing on me, appearing in my mind with different states of being. Each image stays for an unknown period of time with me—maybe one month, maybe longer. Each chooses how and when to appear.

"The first image was Carlos' face as he looked when he died," I continue, making my way to the couch. "It was my company for about one month and was always, absolutely always, on my mind. I admit it was painful to carry him around without his smile and unresponsive to my words. Yet I felt comfortable in his company, knowing he was free. You cannot imagine how much comfort his freedom from pain brought me.

10. *Playful Restorations*

"My inner image of Carlos began changing after my assistant Salu initiated a certain 'game.' It began one evening when I was sitting in the TV room where Carlos and I watched the news. She said: 'Could you both step out of the TV room? I need to vacuum.' I did, and watched her while she went over the area rug. When she was done, she looked at me saying: 'Your chairs are ready. You may both come back now.' I loved every second of the game she created for us—she had been very attached to Carlos for ten years. Our shared fantasy brought him back to life. We talked about how good we felt in our play-acting. One day Salu announced she was going to be in my bedroom. 'Don't look for me, I will be back as soon as I can.' She came out with one of my favorite photographs of Carlos. She had to go through the plastic boxes I store under my bed to find it among hundreds of others; she knew exactly the one she wanted—a large photograph he had taken for professional purposes.

"On my first outing, my first time outside again, I had it framed. He is wearing a dark blue suit, a white shirt, and a light blue tie. It shows him with a calm smile, warm, *simpático,* and wise. If *mensch* had a look, this will be 'it' for me. I placed him on the living room console where he could enjoy the best view—Carlos always looked for the best views, whether in restaurants or theaters. The console allowed him to view the Willamette River, Mount Hood, and, of course, he could also watch me. I said 'hello' and 'goodbye' to him when coming or leaving home; sometimes I kissed him on the lips. In this connecting make-believe of play, Carlos looked at me warmly. I knew it was play and yet my feelings of happiness were real.

"My subjective satisfactions were such that I saw no good reason to stop the 'as if he were alive' game.

"Holding his life-sized portrait allowed me to meet his gaze. When I held the portrait up close, engaging him eye to eye, I could see clearly the lines of warmth imprinted on his face by the passing of time. In the twinkle of his eyes I found his desire to connect with me. I treasured our secret, gaze-to-gaze, intimate moments. I kissed him whenever I wanted. And I felt fine about my incursions in this playful fantasy, as if it were happening in a diluted reality. I continued the game with the photograph by myself, until I came to Buenos Aires."

"He kept you company," suggested Dr. Novelli. "Through this enlivening of the portrait you were working through the trauma of his death, which you couldn't control at the time it happened."

"Yes, but I kept him company too—I did not want him to feel sad or alone. These experiences felt strange to me at times. I had never experienced lapses like them; they had not been part of my personality before Carlos died. But if I had to describe my grief now, I would say that my own process encompassed these slightly strange thoughts and feelings. These playful restorations were a significant part of my grieving, most intensely for about seven months—right up until I boarded Delta flight 110 to come here."

With a gesture, Dr. Novelli invites me to continue.

"Going back to around six months after he died," I add, emending my story, "when my life began resuming old rhythms, I began to forget saying good morning or goodbye to 'Carlos.' I no longer kissed him every day. I forgot to smile to him when I passed by."

I engage Dr. Novelli's kind eyes and confess: "I was afraid. I couldn't tolerate hurting his feelings. Do you remember Becquer's verse 'How sad and alone our loved ones remain'?"

Dr. Novelli: "You seem to be feeling guilty."

"I remember asking myself: 'How can you be such an ungrateful person?' That was guilt, about feeling that I was ungrateful."

I think back on those playful moments, and relive how powerfully real they were. I was fully absorbed in them. They weren't light, like the make-believe games that Salu and I played. I reach inside my purse for a tissue, knowing that my active relationship with the portrait would sound nuts to many. I know it isn't. Dr. Novelli didn't stop to analyze their nuttiness: this tells me he considers them normal in mourning. It was a wonderful space where my incursions into fantasy let me trespass the limits of logic. I could keep Carlos alive at my discretion ... and I could decide when to let him go away—when to let him die.

"Through play," Dr. Novelli says, "you were able to manage the harrowing experience of having him yanked out of your life. Fantasy allowed you to undo the fact that Carlos was dead—he wasn't dead as long as you were playing with him."

"How come his inner picture changes inside me?" I ask.

"Photographs are crutches for our memory," he answers. "They capture a certain moment to make it present. How you felt about the portrait was a reflection of your inner world. You didn't want to abandon the Carlos in the portrait, and you stopped greeting the picture when he started becoming alive inside you. Inside you, he was no longer the deceased Carlos of the picture you carried around at first."

These words assuage my guilt. Dr. Novelli has given a positive twist to my fear of having damaged Carlos with ingratitude. Forlorn, I pause again with my reflections.

"Beatriz," he says, bringing me back to the session, "during one of our past sessions you said—and today you are implying—that you *were afraid to forget Carlos.* Both times you sobbed. 'Forgetting him' means being afraid he would disappear inside you. After the quality bond you and Carlos had for a lifetime, do you think it's even possible he would disappear inside you?"

"I didn't know that six months ago," I reply. "You've made me aware of that a few times, and I am gradually getting it. By the way, Carlos' image in my mind has changed again, here in Buenos Aires, just a week ago."

"Let's see how it changed."

"When I think about Carlos now, I see him happy and alive, surrounded—I mean being climbed on—by our grandchildren. I may frame a photo I have of this happy Carlos with the happy kiddies climbing on him as if he were a tree."

I get lost in my own thoughts, raising questions. Can I regain my old *joie de vivre,* when my major happiness was sharing life with Carlos? How can I do that alone? I would like to believe Carlos is doing well in his afterlife travels. But I can't. Life after death is a concept that eludes and perturbs me. I escape my own thoughts by staring out the window on the left, the one that frames the blue sky and the trees, where small cloud formations go pushed along by the wind.

"Internally," says Dr. Novelli, retrieving me from the heavens, "you have Carlos 'more alive and happier' now."

"I am curious, Dr. Novelli." I don't usually interrupt him. "Do you think that the Carlos 'happy and alive' I see now represents progress on my part? Or am I just in denial of the fact that he is forever gone?"

He is silent. I remain silent too.

"I see a process," he offers, after a long pause, "of going and returning to different life moments. Your election of the last scene with the happy children climbing over him is your return to remembering the vital in Carlos. You are feeling more alive too. I don't see anything pathological."

I breathe a sigh of relief. "That is right, I am feeling more alive, more mobilized now. I am going to the gym. Except Sundays. Working out makes me feel lighter; therapy helps me feel lighter. And I am making progress with my writing again.

"If these out of the ordinary experiences are not pathological," I say, "let me share another. When I was caring for Carlos during the last months of his life, I copied his symptoms. My short-term memory began to fail: I could not remember what I had done earlier in the day; I was losing keys, eyeglasses, books, even the laptop, a relatively large object in an apartment. Losing things had been 'a Carlos exclusive' up until then. Was I showing early signs of Alzheimer's? I even went in for a neurological examination, which was negative. But there were times when the two of us couldn't keep track of doctor's appointments, schedules of medications, and most importantly, doing what we could, preventively, to keep him at the lowest possible pain level. Traumatic stress wilted my attention span: I could attend to only one mission at a time. I was confused under such overload. Seeing my frustration, Carlos gave me loving encouragement: 'You take such good care of me. I am the one who's supposed to take care of you.' After we hired an assistant nurse to make our lives less stressful, my memory returned to normal.

"I identified with him in other ways too, like thinking I had a short life ahead of me. 'Why should I bother going to the gym if I will soon be dead?' 'Why should I study hard to renew my professional license if I will soon be dead?' That obsession with running out of time stayed with me until mid–September. I am realizing now that it evaporated when I stepped onto Argentine soil. I didn't notice its absence until this exact moment."

Engaging the psychologist in me, Dr. Novelli reminds me: "Identifications have a certain function. When you identified with Carlos, you placed him inside you. It was a way to hold on to him."

"Dr. Novelli, I know we have a few minutes left. Let me tell you quickly about the strangest episode I experienced, the only one that worried me as it was happening. Just a few months ago, I was in Portland at the Saturday dance; there was a clothing exchange at the dance that night. I was dancing with a friend when, from a distance, I saw what I thought were Carlos' ties hanging on a rack. How in the world were his ties here? We had given away his old ties in Kansas—before we even moved to Portland. What miracle made them appear 2,000 miles away, not to mention ten years later? Between dances I keep looking at the ties; the designs and colors looked similar in the slightly dimmed light. I overcame an initial reluctance and got closer to the rack, and lifted the ties in my hands: neither the material nor the colors resembled Carlos' ties. I felt relieved. That night I felt strange about this episode and had to give myself a pep talk: *Beatriz, you aren't going crazy: you accepted the reality and did not persist in believing they belonged to Carlos."*

Time is up. I am eager to understand further these episodes, but I will have to do it later. I get up, shake hands with Dr. Novelli, and say goodbye until next week.

After the session I remain self-absorbed, an aura of the surreal hovering in the air around me as I walk. I am unsure about my final destination and walk north along Alcorta Avenue instead of going south in the direction of the apartment. I see Novecento, a fanciful and quiet venue that, despite its smoked glass windows, has a privileged view from inside. I would like to continue my session here. I push the glass door—it doesn't open. Strange. Pressing my nose to the glass I look inside—I see no activity. A tiny sign lets me know the place is *Cerrado por vacaciones* (Closed for vacation). No information about the reopening date. Strange. Since the locale is a large ground floor structure with floor to ceiling windows, maybe the management tried to keep its closure inconspicuous to minimize vandalism.

Since Alcorta is flanked by parks, I take a detour to Libertador Avenue, which has more indoor and outdoor cafés. None of them draw me inside to continue my musings. After a twenty-minute walk, a venue I see from afar draws me over. Eagerly now, I am walking up to Croque Madame, a quaint and relatively quiet café located in the courtyard of the neoclassic Museo de Arte Decorativo. Nestled in its gardens, away from street noise, I sit by the small pond with water lilies. My senses delight in the landscape's French ambience … and it triggers memories of Carlos and me visiting Paris in the heat of summer, strolling along the Tuileries Garden and going to the Musée de l'Orangerie where Claude Monet's water lily murals are.

This twentieth century Museo de Arte Decorativo was the site of one of my first dates with Carlos. He was indeed an adorable romantic. Just last year, not in fantasy but in reality, Carlos and I had lunch here and visited the museum. He told me that back then, he totally made up his mind during our date at this museum that he wanted me to be his wife, and he shared how happy he felt that I emigrated with him and indeed became his wife.

Just eight months before he died, unaware that the end was around the corner, Carlos and I had returned here, where our history as a couple began.

Beautiful memories fill me with joy. I keep thinking about young Carlos who thoughtfully chose the best places to take me on dates. I wish I could hug him now, and with him shed the tears his goodness brings out in me.

It takes time to return to what I came here to think about—my incursions into the zone of fantasy. Slowly sipping an espresso, I begin to transition to the deliciousness of standing between two worlds, having one foot planted in reality and the other in make-believe.

My loss of Carlos—my twin throughout our lifetime together— demolished not just my sense of self, but also tore apart the barrier between reality and fantasy. This is my experience, and I assume that this zone would be known to other mourners—including the families of those buried in Recoleta. Amid the wreckage I discovered a myriad of possibilities which did wonders for working through the trauma of his death: *Carlos didn't really die; I have control over his death; I can let him go; I can bring him back.*

Just as a young child talking with imaginary friends would stop playing if his mother called him, I could stop my make-believe if the phone rang. The analogy to a child reminds me of the child psychoanalyst Donald Winnicott. He described a zone he called an "infinite intermediate" space, where the external and the internal realities coexist. It satisfies me that I've found a theoretical label for my experiences. And I am feeling satisfied to have a name for the space where I enjoyed intimate loving exchanges with Carlos: the *infinite intermediate space.* They were the highlights of my widowhood. They gave wings to my imagination—and set it drifting, in the blue of the skies, like the lilies on a pond.

11

The Anniversary

The slow, instrumental, romantic tangos from the early 1920s like *"Sollozos"* and *"Viaje al Norte"* are a special treat. Since dancers prefer tangos with a strong beat, I don't get to hear these older songs unless I play them at home. Listening, swaying around to the melody, and reading the entertainment section of *La Nación* online, suits me very well this morning. My plan is to lounge at home until I am brave enough or hungry enough—whichever comes first—to emerge from the apartment and step into the outdoor sauna. Staying at home in the steaming metropolis is an escape from temperatures climbing as high as 39°C (102°F) and humidity above 99 percent. In case I have a morning caffeine emergency when housebound, there are instant packets from Starbucks that travel in my suitcase.

During December and January in the Southern hemisphere—the sweltering months of summer—locals file out of the cities in a mass exodus to the beaches of the Atlantic Ocean. As the half-deserted streets stand baking in the heat, the pulse of the city slows. The usual frenzy of cars and pedestrians subsides, and the downtown noise grows fainter. The absence of the locals goes with the shortened entertainment section. Major theater plays and music events tend to relocate temporarily to the popular vacation spots where the locals go: Mar del Plata, Pinamar, and Villa Gessell in Argentina, and Punta del Este in Uruguay—the playground of the jetsetters, the Argentine and European wealthy.

My appetite rises before my courage to venture outdoors, so I put away my CD and stash some money in my purse, and with keys in hand I am ready for the short walk to Café Francesca, which is tucked inside the nearby luxury mall Patio Bullrich. The excellent air

11. *The Anniversary*

conditioning at the mall entices many to go there and spend hours shopping just to enjoy some relief. The number of tables and seats at Francesca lures in those of us who spend long hours at cafés: I see twenty tables available and try one under the natural sunlight streaming through an immense glass cupola and mega chandelier two floors above. After a moment under the torrents of that sunlight waterfall, I get up with my purse and look for a more secluded section, in search of greater privacy. This section behind the mechanical stairs, like a little living room, with tea-colored leather sofas and low coffee tables—this looks like a plush space for my "long term" stay today.

I am trying to like Francesca's atmosphere, but I can't. Do I like the professional servers, with their cordial manners, their black uniforms, and their haste? Do I like the food made far from the eye of a watchful owner who takes pride in quality and freshness? The answers are "no." This is more beautifully appointed and much larger than Dos Escudos, my first love. The line of tango poetry on my mind may be predicting my return: *Siempre se vuelve al primer amor* (You always return to your first love). I had to leave my first love because all of its tables have been full for two weeks in a row.

After trying to like Francesca for about an hour, and not liking it, I finally find one redeeming feature—there is one server unlike the rest. He seems to be out of place here—like me. Could he be missing his former place of work, the way I am missing Dos Escudos? All I know is that under the round cupola, he walks along the periphery of the circular floor as if trying to find something to do. He must be new. Although he can tell by the silverware remaining on my table that another server has already brought my brunch, he comes to my distant sanctuary, leans over my low sofa seat, and inquires softly: "Good afternoon. Are you comfortable?"

"Yes, thank you," I tell him.

"I would be happy to bring you water if the heat has treated you badly."

I accept with a nod of the head and a smile.

"Would you like lemon with your water?"

"Yes! I always welcome lemon."

"Do you prefer lemon slices or lemon juice?"

"Lemon juice would be a luxury, thank you."

"Don't Be Sad When I'm Gone"

He leaves and I muse: water is free, lemon is free—he is respecting my official server's territory by not suggesting items from the menu—he is probably feeling out of place and needs to be useful—he may be a good observer who can tell I am feeling out of place too. Astute eyes would note how I am in my own world by the choice of seating, away from other customers, behind the mechanical stairs, and by the way I am dressed—gym attire at a high-end shopping center—and by what I am doing—typing away on my laptop. Approaching me was his way to converse with someone he imagined to be an oddball like himself. I notice his warmth, his small earrings, his nonlinear speech, and imagine an artist behind the uniform. He brings me the water and lemon juice, plus a glass filled with ice, and stays hanging around while scanning tables in his assigned territory.

After about thirty minutes, we have a minimalistic knowledge of each other—his name is Charly, and this is his first day on the job. He asks what I am writing about, I tell him I am writing a memoir about someone who is his *tocayo* (namesake). In the instant familiarity that develops between strangers in Buenos Aires, I ask what I wouldn't ask in my other culture: "Charly, you don't seem to be a server by profession; what did you do before working here?"

"I am in theater," he says. "I am an actor, but there are no jobs in acting now, so I took this one—temporarily, I hope."

He is an artist—no wonder I sense an affinity. "Oh," I say, "that's why you play the waiter's role so well." We share a laugh.

Sitting near the grand transparent canopy, writing indoors by natural light, and engaging in these exchanges with Charly, the place begins to feel a bit warmer. Charly has begun to build a clientele now, so he is attending several tables nearby. I get up and wave goodbye from afar. He motions me to wait, comes to me, and we depart as good old friends do, with a kiss on the cheek.

I leave the shopping mall and head to my session. Charly or no Charly, I don't imagine returning to Francesca daily. Maybe on occasion.

~~~

As I sit in the corner of my sofa within Dr. Novelli's office, I realize that I've paid no attention to details of the material world around me for the last thirty minutes. Not even when I entered Dr. Novelli's

126

building, rode the elevator up, rang the bell, and greeted him. This total absent-mindedness is uncharacteristic of me.

I start talking.

"Dr. Novelli, early on today I tried to capture the progression of our last session—on December 19—but I can't. And I took no notes of it. I recall saying that Carlos' anniversary was coming up on the 21st. I also recall feeling lazy-minded and sleepy here. Other details are gone, except what you said at the end: 'You are showing signs of anniversary. It may be wise to take it easy today, let yourself feel what comes to you. Don't be afraid of pain.'"

Dr. Novelli lets me know with a gesture that he, too, remembers what he said last session.

"I have been totally absent-minded since I left Café Francesca in Patio Bullrich until I sat down here. I was absent during my five-block walk. My last session is absent too. My unconscious associations today are absences—the missing—the missing Carlos."

Dr. Novelli says nothing so I continue.

"Carlos' anniversary came and went. I was wrong thinking that my emotions would be difficult just on the precise day. Actually, on December 21 I was relatively calm—the entire day. I walked to the synagogue in the morning, had Carlos' family over for dinner, and took several naps in between. The hardest day was the 23rd—after the anniversary had passed."

Dr. Novelli asks, "How was Carlos' family's visit?"

"It was warm and congenial. Counting myself, we were six; counting Carlos, seven. His sister came, with her daughter Roxana, Roxana's husband, and their two teenage children. Roxana was Carlos' close niece, and my faithful support during Carlos' illness; she made the offer to get together the week before. They drove in more than one hour from Ingeniero Maschwitz where they live, so I felt grateful to them for warming up my special day.

"We talked and ate sitting in a circle. When sad memories came up, we put down our utensils and held hands. A sweet empathy connected all of us—including Carlos. I love this family. When we talked about Carlos' suffering at the hands of neglectful doctors, we all got up, opened our arms, and placed each arm around the shoulders of the person on either side. We remembered Carlos in silence, in the circle we formed. Our time together was contented—neither happy nor sad. We were authentic, and honored Carlos' life without fanfare and without getting morose. When someone expressed humor, we laughed. To cap off the evening, we watched a video I had made for Carlos' memorial: *A Life Well Lived*. Everybody enjoyed it."

"How did you feel with Carlos' family?" Dr. Novelli asks.

"Well, this family is loving and gifted at emotional communication in words and actions; it's as easy for them to say 'I love you' as it is to hold hands or to form an embraced circle. All of that warmth brought Carlos' spirit alive for me. Sharing feelings with them was as easy as sharing them with Carlos."

"And your experience at the synagogue?"

"Going to Templo Libertad didn't turn out well. But on my way there, I recovered the most meaningful remembrance of all the travels Carlos and I did together—which were numerous. By most meaningful, I mean the many precious moments we spent together at a faraway temple, in our distant past, in exotic Turkey, where Carlos' father and grandmother were born in the 1800s. Carlos' grandfather had migrated from Russia to Turkey, where he met and married his wife Sara. Years later, Carlos' father Isaac came with his parents to Buenos Aires, thanks to the charity of Baron Rothschild, who financed the emigration of Jews to colonize the Argentine pampas.

"My memories of Etz Ahayim synagogue, located in the Ortakow district of Istanbul, came to me during my forty-five-minute walk to Templo Libertad here. In Turkey, our hotel and the synagogue were near the Bosphorous, the river that connects the Black Sea with the Mediterranean. The sound of names like Etz Ahayim, Ortakow, Bosphorous, and Black Sea fascinate me as much as did the burlap sacks overflowing with colorful spices at the Grand Bazaar.

"But I will come back to the Etz Ahayim story in a moment. First I want to tell you how the idea of going to Turkey developed in Carlos' mind—twenty-seven years ago. Carlos had a penchant for complicated projects; he was made with that inclination. Only he could dream and bring to fruition a project that would take a year to put together. It was 1991. Carlos wanted to join the Turkish Jews' celebration of 500 years of peaceful coexistence in Turkey, which had begun in 1492 when the Sephardic Jews persecuted in Spain were received with open arms by the Turks. To arrange a trip would have been simple. What was challenging was recruiting relatives he had never met who had resided in Paris all their lives—three of his cousins and their wives. Carlos' strong sense of family awoke something in them. They soon decided to make the trip as proposed—to gather in Istanbul in 1992, the eight of us, at an appointed hotel to be chosen on a set day and time convenient for the eight of us, for a two-week celebration vacation. That was the proposal to 'our relatives in Paris,' as Carlos' family referred to them during his childhood. Letters—we didn't use emails then—crossed the Atlantic back and forth, until we all agreed on the details. That's how we met at the lobby of Ciragan Palace Kempinski Istanbul hotel. Carlos was thrilled about meeting them and so was I—call it instant connection or love at first sight. We blended beautifully despite us being a generation younger than them.

"Now back to the temple. Our first family outing was a ten-minute walk from the Ciragan hotel to the Etz Ahayim synagogue. Etz Ahayim had burned in 1941 and was subsequently rebuilt. It was the smallest and least pretentious synagogue façade I had ever seen; in my recollection—maybe distorted by time—its entrance was a narrow gray cement wall with an inconspicuous gray door flanked by two Turkish red flags with their white star and crescent. Security guards came promptly out of nowhere to scrutinize us at the door. Phone calls were made to authenticate our passports.

"Once inside the tiny lobby, women were ushered to watch the ceremony upstairs, and men directed to participate in the service about to start on the ground floor. Etz Ahayim's inside was unassuming, earthy and endearing—unlike the luxury temples I've seen in the United States. From the mezzanine I followed Carlos' movements, my eyes fixed on his back, loving how he looked wearing the *tallit* (white prayer shawl) and the *kippah* (head covering). My heart was fluttering as I was discovering a new side of Carlos as he moved comfortably in front of the altar, in a traditional religious context in front of my eyes. Tall and slender, wearing *kippah* and *tallit* as he looked that day, is how I picture Carlos' spiritual self. On a more recent trip Carlos made to Israel, he purchased a painting that features an older man with a large *kippah* covering his head, praying by the Wailing Wall. The older man in the painting embodies the Carlos I saw in Etz Ahayim."

129

"Don't Be Sad When I'm Gone"

Surprised at the emotions that well up in me as I relate this trip, I look up at Dr. Novelli's eyes and tell him: "What I am going to tell you might make me cry. My throat is in a knot."

Dr. Novelli gestures, encouraging me to go on.

"During this trip, a scientist who lived in Istanbul invited Carlos to give a lecture at Marmara University. Researching its name today, I was reminded that it was Turkey's first medical school—today a global school that teaches in the English language. Carlos' colleague assigned a medical student to show and tell us about the campus with its brick buildings and towers and its unique charm. Watching the two men interact—taking due logical license—I imagined Carlos talking to a younger Carlos from the medical school he would have attended if his grandparents had never emigrated from Turkey to Argentina. A tearful moment for me.

"The lecture in this old house of learning was a trip within a trip. When Carlos first stood at the podium, he expressed gratitude for the invitation, followed by something touching, which I don't remember clearly, something about feeling deeply moved about coming full circle back to the land of his father and his grandmother. Carlos choked a bit during this introduction and dried his tears. We, the audience, dried our tears too.

"There was something universal for me in the story Carlos told, about how we move through time and space, and come back to our roots which may be in strange lands—which turn out to be not strange at all.

"These memories from Turkey, which I recovered while walking to Templo Libertad, were so rich in gratitude and connection, and far more meaningful than my experience at the temple. I had decided to go because Carlos honored his ancestry and had high respect for his lineage.

"I had passed by Templo Libertad many times due to its central downtown location. It isn't a building one just passes by—the structure commands one to stop and admire its massive linear construction which contrasts with its Byzantine façade adorned with Jewish motifs that seem to harbor secret symbols. All done in what looks like filigree carved in stone. I missed seeing the inside of the temple. Through Carlos' eyes—he had gone there by himself—I saw a fascinating gilded sanctuary, extravagant stained-glass windows, and marble sculptures that couldn't be seen from the outside. He commented how different this temple was from the one in the commune of his maternal grandparents, who arrived as rural settlers at a place named Moises Ville, in Provincia de Santa Fe. Are you familiar with the temple?"

Dr. Novelli moves his head affirmatively and says: "Yes, indeed."

"It looked impenetrable—doors closed, no guards. I walked up and down the sidewalk trying to connect with the inside. When I had almost given up, a nondescript building next to it caught my eye; a small sign on its door said: 'Templo Libertad Administrative Offices.' Dialing the intercom in front of cameras on the wall was an unusual experience. Security. The temple's doors were open in the relatively recent past but are sealed today, probably after a terrorist attack at the Argentine Israelite Mutual Association that wounded and killed hundreds. This happened in 1994. A male voice coming through the intercom summoned me to the present: he said visitors could only go inside during service, which were at different hours every day. That was the end of my hope to access the interior, and the end of my desire to connect with the Carlos in *kippah* and *tallit* inside the temple.

"I could not leave yet, since I was feeling tired after my long walk in December's heat and humidity. I spotted a large, low cement structure across the street, in Plaza Lavalle. Could I sit on it, meditate, and connect with Carlos? I crossed Lavalle Street and laid down sideways, facing the temple. From my cement 'couch' I tried to connect with Carlos but got distracted by white clouds moving south over the temple. I lingered, frustrated at not being able to connect with Carlos. My stay ended when two women sat down on the cement couch to talk. Too many distractions."

Dr. Novelli: "That occurred on the 21st of December, on the exact anniversary day. You said that you had unusual experiences on another day."

"Correct. I had an odd episode on the 19th that happened in the calmest of settings. I went to the botanical gardens in search of solace, clean air, and beauty. I must admit I was driven there looking for an encounter with Carlos, and I 'found' him on the spot where he and I recently stood holding hands, looking in awe at the sculpture *Awakening of Nature*, so innocent and so sensuous. This was just last year.

After our connection, I began walking slowly in the shade. Its winding path took me to a site called *Garden of Butterflies,* specially designed to attract butterflies, which don't leave because scientists have chosen plants that offer them food and the right environment for reproduction. I paused to hear the fluttering of their wings as they flew around the Christmas tree there. The sound made me anxious. The surreal in me got engaged—it felt unreal that the butterflies stayed around the tree rather than escaping to the open skies.

"To digress: this morning started with me escaping from the heat outdoors, and with porteños escaping the city; now I am wondering why the butterflies don't escape, since no roof is keeping them there. The mesmerizing scene there reminded me of the surreal Buñuel film *The Exterminating Angel,* where guests at a dinner party retire to the music room of a sumptuous mansion, only to find themselves unable to escape the room. They succumb to anguish; one of them dies, and more eerie details keep unfolding. My anxious inner space saw the butterflies' scene as surreal and connected with the surreal film I saw at least forty years ago. I hear myself referencing the surreal and escaping today.

"Dr. Novelli, my anguish at the botanical gardens generated an imperative need to escape. I ran home from the gardens as fast as I could, rushed to bed, covered myself with blankets, and waited. I felt cold with the air conditioning turned off and under double covers—on a gloriously sunny Sunday afternoon with searing temperatures. I was clearly waiting. Waiting—for what?"

Dr. Novelli: "Beatriz, if you felt cold this summer and stayed under the covers with the air conditioning off, your body was saying something. Only a dead person's body would be cold under those conditions. Through your cold body you were reaching out to Carlos in death. Oftentimes we don't recall a stressful trauma in words, but our body does. The cold 'you' was joining Carlos in his dead state."

"I am remembering something," I say. "Details came to me about the day Carlos died—I had forgotten them until you said what you just said. When he was dead, I covered him up to his neck with a blanket—in case he needed the extra warmth. That's what my body memory did, I was cold and covered by blankets.

"I didn't attribute the oddness to anniversary time: I was thinking

I was incubating an illness. Then my cell phone lit up, and I picked up. It was Gustavo, asking me how I was. 'I have pain in my body and my soul,' I said, using an expression I had never used before. What I said to him means my unconscious knew I wasn't incubating a physical ailment—my 'soul' was hurting."

"You had pain in your body," notes Dr. Novelli, "because you felt alive too; your pain in your soul also means you felt alive. So here is the dual experience of joining Carlos in his dead state intertwined with your certainty that you were alive."

"When Gustavo and I hung up," I continue, "I hid my head under the covers again, and something primary erupted. I cried out loud shouting his name:

Carlos, Carlos, Carlos.
Say something to me!
Send me a sign!
Tell me you where you are.

"I cried the same sounds when Carlos' body was about to be wheeled out of our home in the stretcher, exactly one year and two days before today. Like then, my howling sounds weren't human. Edvard Munch's painting *The Scream* is appearing in my mind. I can hear the 'not fully human' person in the painting howling. Not being heard."

"Somehow," Dr. Novelli observes, "when you get closer to what you call 'the surreal,' you anchor yourself—now in a painting, before in the movie."

"Yes, I don't know why. Munch was quoted as saying that the inspiration for *The Scream* was 'the infinite scream passing though nature.' Could these unfamiliar sounds, mine and Munch's, come from a soul in pain? Shall I go on, Dr. Novelli?"

He nods for me to go on, adding: "You are reliving moments of the day Carlos died, the same 'non-human crying sounds.' This is not unusual at anniversary time."

"Dr. Novelli, more surreal stuff is coming to me—and another painting. I had been preoccupied with the otherworld, ever since Carlos' body was taken out of our home and driven away in the black limousine that disappeared into the black night. Ever since that drizzling dark night, Carlos' new 'residence' had remained an enigma and a curiosity to me. Until last weekend. Gustavo and I went to the William Turner exhibit at the Museo de Bellas Artes. After being apart for several weeks and sharing the hope of a truce and a peaceful afternoon, we had it. We stood before each of Turner's eighty-seven rarely exhibited watercolors, and one of them spoke to me—*Sea and Sky*. It is rounded and serene, with pale oranges and yellows, and lighter whitish tones that fade in the distance. A harmonious and unbounded configuration that suggests the infinite. The sea is a shy grayish-bluish brushstroke that becomes part of the orange. Fluid colors. Merging. No shapes. Just suggestions. I liked it as the habitat where Carlos lives."

After a long silence, Dr. Novelli asks: "What are you thinking about?"

"I am thinking that every day is anniversary day. That maybe there is a 'forever' embedded in grief.

"There are daily perceptions, sensations, emotions originating in me or in others that trigger memories of something or other that Carlos and I did together—that trigger tears of sadness or gratitude and make me feel that I am honoring him.

"Our two weeks in Turkey in 1992 opened my life to another family, another time and space, a universal dimension. Today I hear something in Carlos' words there, in the land where his family originated, where he was embraced so warmly at the podium of the University of Marmara Medical School. And the painting Carlos brought from Israel attests to that lineage chain; the man at the Wailing Wall, he represents Rabbi Dujovne of Odessa—the beginning of the Dujovne lineage according to family records. Carlos' last name, Dujovne, means 'spiritual man.'

"I contemplate the metaphor of Carlos completing a cycle when he died. It will be my turn to complete my own cycle––I won't have the prolific family he had. But if I was ever afraid of death, I know how to do that now—Carlos taught me to fight for life as long as it is reasonable, and then to let go. As the Rabbi Cahana in Portland once said to me, 'Carlos continues to teach us.'"

12

A Colorful Carlos Day

Returning to Portland is on my mind.

On my way to Buenos Aires, I knew my day-to-day life would carry a certain task: placing myself out of my comfort zone, to learn who I am without Carlos by my side. I look back to see whether I have really done this and what my voyage has taught me.

Fully ready to go out, I secure the apartment and descend to the ground floor thinking about the unquestionable assertiveness that marked me since I was a child, and about my self-effacing behavior in this time of grief. At the door, I take a moment to decide whether I want to go right on Montevideo towards Dos Escudos or left towards Café Francesca. I haven't seen Charly in a week and feel like chit-chatting with him, but I also carry the laptop in my oversized bag in case I want to write.

I scan the streets and see them relatively empty. The taxis that pass me by are not carrying passengers. There are no customers in the shops I pass. The energy of the city at its lowest. New York empties in the heat of August, Buenos Aires empties in the heat of January and February. Most people are still fleeing these humid 100-degree days for the beaches and resorts along the Atlantic coast. Vacationing on the beach is a necessity for locals; when I was a child and lived here, we used to go to Mar del Plata. The nearest beaches are a five-hour drive south of the city. Families that can afford a costly vacation leave for one month or longer. Those who can't afford a vacation take the overnight train or bus or drive their cars for a long weekend.

I choose a seat at Francesca under the glass dome, in Charly's serving area. We spot one another and smile and wave. The place is busier than usual so it takes him a while to come and take my order.

Besides, Charly is now being sought out by clients who like his service and come back to him.

I inspect the dome above Francesca that pokes above the mall to the outdoors. Then, with eyes adjusting, I look through the glass panels facing the interior, and see the entrance to my gym Life Center Elegance, on the third floor of Patio Bullrich. I smile remembering how I met a friend there—this would have never happened if I had not challenged myself to operate outside my shrinking comfort zone. It happened several months ago: I was on the treadmill when I saw him from afar, tall, beautiful, wearing a thin electric-blue bodysuit that fit him like a second skin.

This contemporary Michelangelo's *David* broke the monotony of my workout. Photographers joined him to take pictures as he leaped between exercise machines, bars, and scaffolding to land with perfect equilibrium in poses that only ballet dancers would be capable of doing with such agility and elegance. It was as natural to take photos of this living marvel as it was to take snapshots of the actual *David* I saw when I was in Florence once. With trepidation I approached this walking blue sculpture and asked permission to take a photo. Up close, I observed the contour of every muscle in his body, as I did in front of the real *David*. This was no physical or animal attraction. Beauty can be no less compelling.

"Good morning, my name is Beatriz Dujovne. May I take pictures along with your photographers?" He hesitated a bit and nodded me a yes with a shy smile. He did not say his name.

"He is a famous personality. The photos you are taking are worth a lot of money," said one of the men. I said I didn't live in Buenos Aires and did not know many public figures.

"You have to be a classical dancer," I said to him.

"I dance everything," he answered with a big smile.

To find a common ground, I said I had seen several Argentine ballet dancers in the United States, where I live. I mention Bocca, Guerra, Cornejo, Herrera…. "Hernan Piquín is one of my favorites—I saw him interpreting Freddy Mercury. He was too much!"

He seemed pleased that I am not foreign to his world. From this beginning our smooth friendship developed. I was curious about his life in Buenos Aires, and he was curious about my life in the United

States. We coordinated our schedules to do our daily treadmill work-outs at the same time. We got to know the details of our lives "tread-milling" thirty minutes a day, Monday through Saturday. His name is Joel. He was a former dancer of the Argentine TV series *Dancing for a Dream*. He is into astrology, so early on, he asked when my birthday was. On my birthday he surprised me with an invitation to a dinner party for me at his apartment, when he found out I was going to be alone in the evening. I was pleased to be in his company outside the gym, and to enjoy his friends' company on my special day. I felt love at first sight with all of them—renowned designers in the *haute couture* world of Argentina. They poured affection on me. It was a balm to re-ceive this warmth after months of bad blood with pouncing Gustavo. The nice connection with Joel and his talented friends would not have happened without Dr. Novelli pointing out—over and over again—the negative dynamics of my friendship with Gustavo, and his suggestions that I select friends with positive energy.

Charly comes rushing over to take my order.

"I am sorry, Bea," he says, "I am a little disorganized today, I feel so excited! I will tell you all about it when the lunch crowd leaves."

"No worries, Charly," I reply. "I was going through memories of how I met Joel—do you remember him?" He doesn't. "I introduced the two of you about three weeks ago; we were sitting in the sofas behind the stairs. He is the TV dancer that comes to the gym upstairs."

"Oh ... yes, Bea, I remember him. I was sorry I could not spend time with you and him that day. I had to check in for work," says Charly.

"Charly, let me not detain you. I will have baked salmon, and a salad. As an appetizer I would like the double macchiato I haven't had today." Smiling, I add, "As presto as possible, Charly."

Gracious Charly takes the order to the kitchen and dashes back with the double coffee. We share our news fast, since he does not have the freedom to talk too long with customers—Francesca does not en-courage leisure among its staff. It doesn't buy newspapers for the cus-tomers either. The management keeps an eye on the servers. Between Charly's trips to the kitchen, he tells me how excited he is about leaving for the beach tonight. He will catch the overnight bus after his finishes work at 8. Early tomorrow he will be in Santa Teresita, at a five-star hotel he booked with a huge discount. He will be at the beach on Saturday and Sunday, then the overnight bus will bring him back to Buenos Aires in the morning so he can report to work by noon Monday. Charly does not mind the stress and time it takes to get there. I begin to understand all over again how much a trip to the beach means to my compatriots.

"Bea, I want so badly to go away, just to stare at the ocean, hear the murmur of the waves, meditate, feel part of the universe, and nourish my spirit."

"You poet! If you get all that out of the ocean, it's worth going even for one hour."

I eat the surprisingly delicious salmon and we kiss goodbye until next week, wishing each other a good weekend.

On the way to therapy, I pass a fruit vendor on the street, tending an exquisitely arranged extra-large woven tray. I know his fruit is fresh and has the best taste, so I buy oranges, strawberries, pears, and grapes. Will the handles of the plastic bag he gave me be strong enough to carry this heavy purchase? I ask for a double bag just in case and resume my walk.

I still have six blocks ahead of me. I hurry up and get there exactly on time, but alas! The doorman tells me there is no electricity in the neighborhood, no bell sound to announce my arrival to Dr. Novelli, and of course no functioning elevators either. He complains about the hardships caused by frequent *apagones* (electrical shortages) in the city. I approach the dark service stair and feel dismayed with my leather bag holding the laptop and the plastic bag with three kilos of fruit. I need an extra hand for my cellular: I must illuminate the steps with the flashlight. Did I have to buy fruit today? With an unequal weight in each arm, I begin the ascent and feel overchallenged trying to climb three floors while figuring out how to position my feet on the odd-shaped narrow steps. I hear a person behind me unable to pass me: it's a man in his forties. Since I feel Buenos Aires is a large family, given my seniority, I ask him to please carry one of my bags. He offers to carry both, and we begin to make our progress faster together.

I knock on Dr. Novelli's door, which is partly open due to the *apagón,* and he welcomes me to an office that, with the light coming in through the window on the left, is not even any darker than usual.

≈≈≈

"Dr. Novelli, I want to tell you about Sylvia, my new friend. It has been so easy to get along with her. A respite from my struggles to get along with Gustavo."

Dr. Novelli smiles.

"We go back to Buenos Aires in 2016. She was in the periphery of my life then. She met Carlos when the three of us went to the Torquato Tasso music club to see Rodolfo Mederos, the *bandoneón* player. During the pre-show dinner, we had plenty of time for conversation; Carlos and Sylvia told me, after the show was over, how much they liked meeting each other. In October 2017, she came to the Portland Tango Festival. Chatting at our shared table beside the dance floor, I mentioned I would be in Buenos Aires the following year, and she arranged her trip to overlap with mine. This year she became the center of my social life. While Gustavo and I were engaged in hellish battles, she and I spent easy times together. We arranged joint outings around our busy lives with no trouble at all.

"I sensed our lives would be intertwined for years to come. I just did, even though we were frequent travelers, and she lived by the Atlantic Ocean and I lived by the Pacific Ocean. We met in September when Buenos Aires had optimal temperature and luminosity. We waited for the *Jacarandá* trees to show off their light purple flowers that tint the city for about a month. It was nice to be with her, sharing commentaries about the life renewal of the season.

"Now that I have given you our background, our outing last week will make more sense. Before she was due to depart, we were leisurely sitting under the outdoor pink umbrellas of La Panera, sipping a concoction of grapefruit, ginger, and mint that is so refreshing in this summery January weather. Sylvia got excited and said: 'Why don't we have an all Carlos day? We can go to his favorite places, do the activities he liked, and eat his favorite foods.' With our joint creativity, we planned it for Sunday, the day before she was scheduled to leave. We met at 2 p.m. and finished our day eight hours later.

"I must digress a little: Being with another person for eight hours

139

is a record for me. Deep down I am an introvert who can easily switch to extroversion—for short periods. She has a similar configuration of introversion and extroversion.

"We started where Carlos used to begin his day, at Confitería La Biela. I was waiting on the sidewalk when she arrived in a taxi. I said that for our plan to be fantastic it would require Miguel serving tables on Sunday. We walked up and down La Biela outdoors hoping to see Miguel. We did, although he typically doesn't work on Sundays. I saw him serving outdoor tables. I ask Sylvia to sit in his area and wait for me. I walk toward Miguel. He is carrying a large tray to a table where a big party sits. Shall I interrupt him? I do and whisper my plan in his ear. I got his answer immediately—a big smile and raised eyebrows. After delivering the tray, he would join us. Miguel was happy to participate in the Carlos Day, since he and Carlos, who had known each other for ten years, shared a current of mutual affection. I signal to Sylvia that Miguel is 'on.' We smile at the news. Miguel comes to our table and kisses Sylvia on the cheek, just because she is my friend. I so enjoy the kissing part of La Biela's culture. I don't know if you have noticed that it is one of the most expensive eating-places in Recoleta; the food is not that good, but customers keep coming for its location and the professional servers that have been there for decades. Not only are they skillful at remembering large orders without taking notes, they also share a current of affection with the habitués."

Dr. Novelli smiles and nods in agreement with my opinions.

"The plan, I tell Miguel, is to order the *Gancia* with soda, ice, and lemon—exactly the way Carlos liked. We also want a *picada*. I explain to Sylvia that *picada* is a tray with several subdivisions for small food bites that you pick up with forks or toothpicks. Carlos used to drive Miguel insane asking him to bring as many individual dishes as possible with Florentine tripe—everybody gets no more than one. Carlos wanted warm black olives—not the green ones everybody gets. Miguel loved pleasing Carlos sometimes with four or six little plates of tripe and never failing to bring the warm olives. Carlos loved to tip Miguel excessively. The *picada* was the first experience for Sylvia. I thought she would like it since she is used to European foods. It takes her a while to decide she would try the tripe; when she does, she can't help but say she loves the sauce, she likes the tripe.... But 'no more, thank you' because tripe is the lining of the stomach and it grosses her out. We are done. Where would Miguel be to say good-bye? We waited for him listening to *'Con te partirò'* (I'll go with you) by a street violinist. This romantic and poignant funeral song was the ultimate gift to Carlos on his day. He and I listened to Andrea Bocelli and Sara Brightman singing it. We found Miguel, kissed him goodbye, and thanked him for the comradery after this midday appetizer and a few Carlos stories.

"We began to cross the plaza to our two next 'Carlos' stops. Honoring our introverted needs, we walked in silence under the sun for around ten minutes until we reached the north side of the park, next to Recoleta cemetery. Our destination is Centro Cultural Recoleta (CCR), another Carlos favorite, to take photographs. 'Are you interested, Sylvia?' She is always interested. We are still maintaining our restorative silence. I guided her to the terraces there, painted in bright yellow-ochre alternating with dull brick. Carlos admired the aesthetics that combine classic sculptures, modern lines, warm colors, and plants. The shrubbery in several shades of green invites my embrace, literally. Instantly Sylvia is in photography-heaven. She took pictures of me being silly, hugging plants, shrubs, the wind, and even the blue skies. I photographed her being silly too. We are in extroversion mode being giddy. 'I will take you through some passages and hallways to get to an exhibit that has been prepared just for me! *Films in the Mind: Psychology and Cinema Since Sigmund Freud.*'—'I am following you, Beatriz.' It's small and charming. We delight in the air of mystery and the most unusual set-up. There are three films projected in separate areas of a single space. In front of one of them, I explain to Sylvia, a fainting couch and a chair have been placed as they would be in a psychoanalytic consulting room: the chair is behind the couch; the analyst sees the patient, but the patient does not see the analyst. The rationale for this arrangement is to foster the patient's regression and the process of free association without interference of the analyst in his visual field. I lie on the couch, Sylvia sits on the chair behind the couch, and we watch the film—a sequence of several excerpts from movies where patients and analysts are in session. I am enchanted in this setting and ask Sylvia to take my picture from her vantage point showing me lying on my back, making sure my feet are in the photograph. I made a note of the films to watch at home at a later time: *Carefree, Spellbound, What about Bob, Annie Hall, Bridget, Prime.*

"We leave the CCR, Sylvia walking ahead of me towards the façade of the colonial Iglesia del Pilar. Her voice at full volume is urging me to walk faster: 'Hurry up, Beatriz! Look up to the campanile: you see the rainbow that just appeared around it? It is Carlos, he is watching us, he feels happy we are remembering him like this.'

"Indeed. Around the cupola, a beautiful rainbow with unusually bright colors—as if illuminated by a gigantic flash—was finding its way between layers of gray and white clouds. We watched it, mesmerized. In real time, I sent photos to the family sharing the experience Sylvia discovered, and what she had said.

"As nothing else could top this experience, we decided to stop for the afternoon. It was getting close to Sylvia's dinnertime—not mine. She is on European or U.S. time, depending on where she came from, and I am fully on Argentine time. We negotiated to eat at 7:30, which is late for her and early for me. To negotiate with Sylvia is always easy. My apartment was just four blocks away, handy for taking the power nap we both needed."

"How were you feeling about this experience, Beatriz?" asks Dr. Novelli.

"To negotiate with Sylvia was easier than negotiating with myself. Of course, I kept comparing the smoothness of being with Sylvia to the tumultuousness of being with Gustavo.

"We felt sufficiently restored after a one-hour nap, and more than ready to walk six blocks to Carlos' favorite Italian restaurant. I had made reservations at Sottovoce although reservations are not needed before 9. I reserved 'Carlos' and my table,' the third in the intimate upstairs seating, closer to the stairs. Sylvia responded with a 'wow' to the overall casual elegance of the place. Inside myself I was with Carlos, feeling his vibrations. We were led to the exact table I had requested. The same welcoming champagne that Carlos and I used to drink was brought to our table immediately and we consumed it right away. Now giggling, since we don't normally consume alcohol, we savored cold hors d'oeuvres, examining the color and texture, and commenting on the taste of every bite—all real Italian and real tasty. We spent some time choosing what to order next because everything on the menu was

Carlos' favorite. We settled on *pappardelle alla Bolognese* with cream of mushrooms, which arrived in twenty minutes, as it should when pasta is homemade and cooked *al dente*. It was hilarious to watch Sylvia's delight before she even took a bite of pasta. She moaned and groaned, swearing it was the best she ever had. She didn't want dessert. I didn't either, but I explained it would not be a 'Carlos day' without their Italian pannacotta—not only Carlos' absolute favorite among all desserts, but also his very favorite pannacotta among all the ones he tried. Sylvia didn't even want to look at the dessert menu until she saw the delicate white custard-looking dessert with designs on the plate made of strawberry sauce and bits of caramelized orange peel. The waiter centered the luscious looking tray on the table, with a second spoon calling her name. She happily surrendered to the calling, tried the pannacotta and went to heaven."

Dr. Novelli: "How did you feel during the Carlos day?"

"It was like being with Carlos," I say, impressing myself with how fast I answered his question. I had not entertained such a thought before. I pause.

"You seem to have something on your mind," says Dr. Novelli.

"I was thinking about how fast I responded to your question. Sylvia is a generous and kind person. Her spontaneous gift pleased me so much that I didn't know how to thank her."

"You are assuming she did all of this as a present to you," suggests Dr. Novelli. "What if she did it to please herself too?"

"I took it as a selfless act," I respond. "I am used to Carlos being one-hundred percent selfless with me."

Dr. Novelli signals me to go on.

"She talks more than I do, which was the case with Carlos too. With Carlos and Sylvia, the conversation is of mutual interest. Sylvia is independent like Carlos was, and when she comes back from her adventures, she likes to share them. Carlos and I focused our time on personal projects we shared when we came together. I am drawing parallels."

Dr. Novelli's facial expression tells me he is about to challenge me: "When you meet people, you compare them with the model of Carlos you carry inside. I've seen you do this with both men and women, Beatriz."

143

"I do. After spending my entire life with Carlos … doesn't it make sense to be drawn to people that feel like him? Do you see a problem I don't see?"

"Attributing Carlos' characteristics to others, who don't have them, is an illusion you create for yourself," says Dr. Novelli. "From illusion you have no choice but to end up in disillusionment. Doing this would set off a chain of illusions and disillusions in you. Being open to meet people without expecting them to be like Carlos would be better."

As I do after most sessions, I feel grateful that Dr. Novelli sees so much more inside me than I can see on my own. He leaves me with much to ponder at the end of this session.

I pick up my two heavy bags, one in each hand, so we say goodbye without shaking hands. He opens the door, and from the natural light of his office, I see a hallway dimmer than usual. The electricity has not come back. I turn my phone flashlight on and alternate safety calculations with brief movements down the steps.

Once outside, I resume my inner dialogue. It is common to project onto others the emotions we cannot tolerate inside ourselves, like anger or envy, but Dr. Novelli told me I've been projecting goodness onto others, Carlos' goodness. I see his point, with a caveat. It could be good to see others in a better light, as long as I am aware of what I am doing. If I go unaware of my proclivity to project this way, which I didn't know I was doing until today's session, it could put me at risk of being emotionally confused, of not seeing people as they are.

Exhausted from overthinking it, and from carrying my laptop and the bag of fresh fruit, I get to my apartment building and smile when I look up to see the lights on.

Epilogue:
One Year Later

My nine-hour stop in Atlanta came to an end with the loudspeakers announcing that the Boeing 767 to Buenos Aires was ready to begin boarding.

After a combined twenty-three hours of ground and air travel from Portland to Buenos Aires, I couldn't get out of the plane fast enough. I was squeezing my carry-on and ready to walk before the wheels even hit the ground. When it was okay to unbuckle and move around the cabin, I leaped out of my seat and positioned myself swiftly by the exit door; I got out of the plane in seconds, and in no time I had crossed the terminal and sailed past the immigration checkpoint.

Approaching baggage claim, I thought of how impossible it would be to find that sweet young porter Pedro again when I spotted him hanging around the carrousel.

"Buen día, Pedro, how are you? You helped me last year."

"How are you? I remember you," he said.

"Could you help me get through customs and take me to the Airport Taxi Company? I made a reservation from the United States."

I didn't handle Pedro's tip the way Carlos taught me, but I trusted that my decision to not show him the tip in advance was fine with honest Pedro.

I felt a pang in my gut as we crossed the lobby and passed the spot where my old friend was waiting for me last year. He was the major trauma during my stay in Buenos Aires, but at least I succeeded in saying "no" to him before that trip was over. To arrive this time with no one waiting for me, upon reflection, felt liberating.

Epilogue: One Year Later

Pedro carried out his job to perfection. He walked me to the taxi fleet and sought out the chauffeur assigned to my reservation. I smiled at the little white square taxicabs that looked like they belonged in an amusement park. I gave Pedro his tip with a kiss on the cheek and said goodbye until sometime soon.

As the white amusement-park car drove me from Ezeiza airport into the city, I thought about how different the flight had been from the one last year. The jumbo jet was just a flying machine this time, a commercial airliner for adults. It was no emergency hospital for my broken heart; the round headboards were light gray rather than hospital-white; the seats were not cribs for sick children; and there were no nurses descending from heaven to safeguard my sleep or to offer me potions to soothe my nerves. The workers passing out wine and spirits were just hurried flight attendants, following their routines in a mostly timely manner.

As the cab weaves through traffic and horns blare nearby, it dawns on me that the thought of my own death no longer frightens me. I recognize how much I have grown into being a woman alone in the world.

We reach the same apartment Carlos and I had rented for several years, the same one I rented last year, the one on Montevideo Street, with the balcony where the mating doves performed their squawking ritual dance. I keep glancing at the window beside the balcony as I unpack my luggage. Mating season is over by now. And as I reach down for an armful of blouses and turn around to the closet, I see a baby dove, perched on the windowsill, inside. Looking past it to the trees behind, I can see its parents watching from afar. The baby pecks the sill, shows me a cute 360-degree turn, and flies away zealously followed by mom and dad.

I have returned to this Recoleta neighborhood in search of *affinity*, the new living compass I've developed during my second year without Carlos. With this inner sensor for guidance, I can better follow my own subtle advice. Affinity tells me whether places and people are good for me. When I sense lack of affinity, I withdraw. I feel total affinity walking along the wide streets and avenues here with their full view of the blue skies I think about when I am not here. And those institutions of my personal connection are here too: Café Dos Escudos and Café La Biela. They are essential for my wellbeing every single day of my stay.

Recoleta feeds my needs for familiarity and belonging. There is a sweetness in being acknowledged and recognized many times a day, a sweetness in giving the same recognition to others. Little things matter: the exchange of gazes, warm greetings, being called by my name—all of it balances my excessive abstract life online. I am referring to exchanges with semi-anonymous people, like servers at restaurants and shop owners. Most of the professional servers at La Biela, who started working there forty years ago, haven't changed in decades—customers are loyal to this business for their connection with servers and the recognition they get from them. Dos Escudos, my other working and connecting café, employs younger servers who are more mobile; three of them I got to know last year left while I was in Portland. I miss the rapport I had with them.

With Mario the shop owner who repairs shoes, I have a connection just from patronizing his shop for twelve years. Right before I returned to the United States in February of last year, I found his shop closed. The shut door felt ominous then, so this year, before taking my tango heels to Mario, I asked Julio—the shoeshine man—if he had any news about Mario. The good news, he said, is that he is back at work after heart surgery; the bad news is that he is still smoking and does it in hiding.

In the United States I don't have to worry about good and bad cleaners: no cleaners I've ever used can get stains out; I ask them why they are in the business if they cannot clean soiled clothes and I usually get just a look. In Recoleta, I know which cleaners don't take stains out of clothes, so I go to one that does. Recoleta is also home to Isaac, my hairdresser of twelve years whose creativity goes beyond hair styling—he sings, paints oils, and tells stories. In the past, after my weekly hairstyle appointment, I used to go home and tell Isaac's funny stories to Carlos. I couldn't tell them with much grace, but Carlos could recycle them with the right sense of timing and suspense.

All my days this past year have begun as a tabula rasa, a blank slate. Today does too. It is my birthday.

Epilogue: One Year Later

As I rise and connect with my physical environment, inner sensors message me. They tell me what suits me at the moment. Mornings and afternoons unfold organically—not forced one way or another by habit. For someone whose professional day was ruled by the fifty-minute therapy hour for thirty years, designing the day as I go is satisfying and freeing. It's a "no" to scheduled time.

No one offered to celebrate my birthday; no gatherings, no coffees, no dinners show up in my calendar. It's atypical, but I note it as a fact without feeling sorry for myself. This is my first *re-birthday,* for my separate self, after the demolition of my joint life with Carlos. He would have surprised me today; the last card he gave me had a photograph of two toddlers, a boy and a girl sitting next to each other, kissing delicately on the lips as the boy holds her face tenderly with his plump hand. Carlos handwrote: "This tenderness reminds me of our first kiss." He would have chosen a unique place for dinner. I see green gardens ... a sign that I will take myself out—for breakfast!

Park Hyatt Buenos Aires Hotel. I get there in no time since it is just around the corner, on Montevideo and Alvear. Excited about attending my own grand event, I cross the lobby to reach the outdoor gardens. This is a stately and grand neoclassical palace built in the early 1930s. As Carlos and I did once, I skip the elevator and climb three levels of fifty concrete steps—platforms laid out on a perfectly manicured green hill of terraces and courtyards. Each level features a different restaurant. I sit at an outdoor table in the shade on the third floor. The server asks if there is a special occasion. "Yes," I smile, "I am replicating a birthday my husband gave me here three years ago. He isn't with me now." She nods without comment, and in short order breakfast is served and enjoyed. At the end of the meal, she brings out a chocolate pastry called "Snickers Tarta," made with chocolate, marshmallow cream, caramel, salted peanuts, and a chocolate caramel frosting—with an elongated white candle sticking out of the top. I ate it all.

After breakfast I take the stairs back down and head to a session with Dr. Novelli. I greet him with a kiss on the cheek and plop down into the same old corner of the moss green couch. I am beaming today. He finds the story of today's birthday a gold mine. He sees it as a symbol of my recovered self-esteem. A significant change, he notes; it marks a new sense of independence. I am no longer entertaining a fantasy about being incomplete without Carlos. To me, the event seems neither happy nor unhappy. It is what it is. It's just how I am now.

With therapy comes self-knowledge. That helps us take ownership of our projections. My problems with tango last year, which pained me so deeply, gradually eased as my self-esteem recovered and I got away from toxic company. Therapy threw light on how things were interconnected, and how I couldn't resolve one without resolving the other. It was a balancing act of many interacting forces with roots in the unconscious. When I left Buenos Aires, my inner emotional changes became manifested in self-enhancing thoughts and behaviors. Last year I went tiptoeing around undeserving people; today I enjoy saying "no" to them.

I was surprised by how much I enjoyed dancing tango in Portland. I liked the tango people in Portland much more than their counterparts in Buenos Aires, who viewed me as an outsider. What a paradox! Now, during this second year in Buenos Aires, I've made friends with tango. I've had sweet experiences. Like when a stranger whose name I don't know began crying on my shoulder while we were dancing. He explained he couldn't control his tears due to the recent death of his wife, who was also his dance partner. He apologized, but I told him I was glad he'd found a safe place to cry.

Another dance partner, Roberto, told me he was 83 and the widow of a wife he adored who had died several years ago. Two weeks later, at the same venue, Roberto told me he was 77 and that he would like to have a relationship with me off the dance floor and "beyond the libido." In a friendly manner, I told him to quit the advances and complimented him for "beyond the libido," a creative expression on his part. He had small dancing eyes, and was prone to laugh like I am, so ours was a mixture of a funny and a serious exchange. He wouldn't let go of the thread: "Wouldn't it be nice to go out to a museum exhibit, have a nice dinner, and do wonderful outings 'beyond the libido'?" The punch line was yet to come. "In the winter," he continued, "we could lie down together and warm each other's feet." This scene struck me as hilarious and I laughed and he laughed before I left. That's how we navigated out of a strangely cute exchange.

Epilogue: One Year Later

I was glad to laugh on the same dance floors that I hated so much last year. Where I used to scan the room with a scowl, I found myself dancing with men who had the most pleasant and outgoing personalities. Fernando, for example, who every time he led a complex move which I was able to follow, would say: "That's it, Beatriz," or "Brava, Beatriz," or "What a wonder, the way you dance, Beatriz."

Were these pleasant men here last year? I suspect they were, just as I was, but they were probably repelled by my anger at their machismo. Therapeutic epiphanies were necessary to change my relationship with tango.

I even went back to dance classes, at a school with talented teachers in their thirties. The old-timers usually put down such places out of envy. I requested the teacher Pedro, with whom I had the best rapport last year. When he saw me at the appointed time, he gave me a big hug and said he was happy to see the queen of the dance halls. He remembered the bad times I had last year. Before teaching me, he said, he wanted to dance a few songs. We did.

"Your dance is on a different planet this year. You followed everything I led. You feel secure, you feel light. Your balance has improved one-hundred percent. Now: we are going to refine some things...."